GW00418789

Cycle TOURS

Around London North

Nick Cotton

First published in 2002 by
Philip's, a division of
Octopus Publishing Group Ltd
2-4 Heron Quays
London E14 4JP

First edition 2002
First impression 2002

Based on the original Ordnance Survey Cycle Tours series
first published by Philip's and Ordnance Survey®.

ISBN 0-540-08192-2

The route maps in this book are reproduced from
Ordnance Survey® Landranger® mapping.

Text and compilation copyright © Philip's 2002

Ordnance Survey®

This product includes mapping data licensed from Ordnance
Survey® with the permission of the Controller of Her Majesty's
Stationery Office. © Crown copyright 2002. All rights reserved.
Licence number 100011710

Photographic acknowledgements

AA Photo Library 19, 49, 55, 67, 89, 113, 117, 121 • Nick
Cotton 61, 85, 100, 105, 109 • Andy Williams 24, 37

Contents

Abbreviations and symbols

Directions

L	left
R	right
LH	left-hand
RH	right-hand
SA	straight ahead or straight across
T-j	T-junction, a junction where you have to give way
X-roads	crossroads, a junction where you may or may not have to give way
'Placename 2'	words in quotation marks are those that appear on signposts; the numbers indicate distance in miles unless stated otherwise

Distance and grade

The number of drink bottles indicates the grade:

Easy
Moderate
Strenuous

The grade is based on the amount of climbing involved.

Refreshments

Pubs and teashops on or near the route are listed. The tankard ♥ symbols indicate pubs particularly liked by the author.

Page diagrams

The page diagrams on the introductory pages show how the map pages have been laid out, how they overlap and if any inset maps have been used.

This section of the route is shown on pages 20 and 21

This overlap area appears at the foot of pages 20 and 21 and at the top of pages 22 and 23

This section of the route is shown on pages 22 and 23

Richmond

This area is shown as an inset on page 21

Cross-profiles

The vertical scale is the same on each diagram but the horizontal scale varies according to the length of the route.

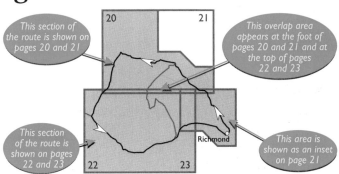

Sychnant Pass

Cefn Coch

Rowen

Start/finish

Start/finish

Legend to 1:50 000 maps

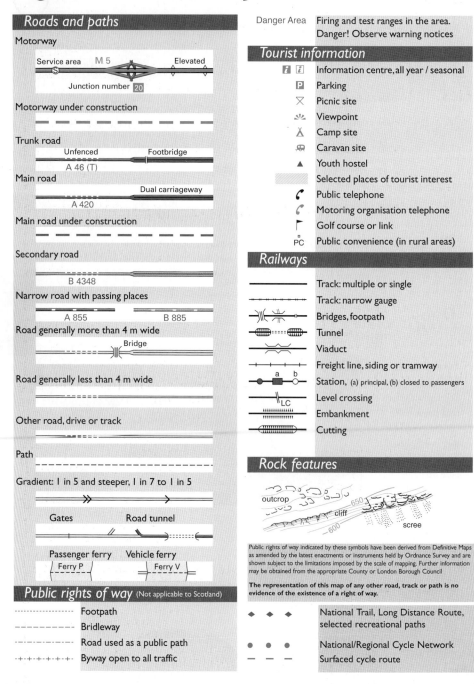

Roads and paths

Motorway

Service area   M 5   Elevated

Junction number   20

Motorway under construction

Trunk road
Unfenced   Footbridge
A 46 (T)

Main road
Dual carriageway
A 420

Main road under construction

Secondary road
B 4348

Narrow road with passing places
A 855   B 885

Road generally more than 4 m wide
Bridge

Road generally less than 4 m wide

Other road, drive or track

Path

Gradient: 1 in 5 and steeper, 1 in 7 to 1 in 5

Gates   Road tunnel

Passenger ferry   Vehicle ferry
Ferry P   Ferry V

Public rights of way (Not applicable to Scotland)

················ Footpath
‑ ‑ ‑ ‑ ‑ ‑ ‑ Bridleway
‑·‑·‑·‑·‑· Road used as a public path
‑+‑+‑+‑+‑+‑ Byway open to all traffic

Danger Area   Firing and test ranges in the area. Danger! Observe warning notices

Tourist information

ℹ ℹ   Information centre, all year / seasonal
P   Parking
✕   Picnic site
⥾   Viewpoint
⅄   Camp site
⌂   Caravan site
▲   Youth hostel
      Selected places of tourist interest
☏   Public telephone
☏   Motoring organisation telephone
⌐   Golf course or link
PC   Public convenience (in rural areas)

Railways

—————   Track: multiple or single
++++++ Track: narrow gauge
        Bridges, footpath
        Tunnel
        Viaduct
++++++ Freight line, siding or tramway
  a b
        Station, (a) principal, (b) closed to passengers
  LC   Level crossing
        Embankment
        Cutting

Rock features

outcrop
cliff   650
600   scree

Public rights of way indicated by these symbols have been derived from Definitive Maps as amended by the latest enactments or instruments held by Ordnance Survey and are shown subject to the limitations imposed by the scale of mapping. Further information may be obtained from the appropriate County or London Borough Council

The representation of this map of any other road, track or path is no evidence of the existence of a right of way.

◆ ◆ ◆   National Trail, Long Distance Route, selected recreational paths
● ● ●   National/Regional Cycle Network
— — —   Surfaced cycle route

4

Water features

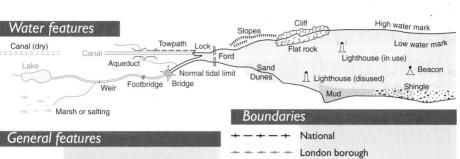

Canal (dry)
Lake
Canal
Aqueduct
Towpath
Lock
Ford
Weir
Footbridge
Bridge
Normal tidal limit
Marsh or salting

Slopes
Cliff
High water mark
Flat rock
Sand Dunes
Low water mark
Lighthouse (in use)
Beacon
Lighthouse (disused)
Mud
Shingle

General features

⋏——⋏——⋏	Electricity transmission line (with pylons spaced conventionally)
> – –> – – >	Pipeline (arrow indicates direction of flow)
⌐ruin	Buildings
	Public buildings (selected)
▬	Bus or coach station
	Coniferous wood
	Non-coniferous wood
	Mixed wood
	Orchard
	Park or ornamental grounds
	Quarry
	Spoil heap, refuse tip or dump
Ⱦ	Radio or TV mast
∎	Church or chapel with tower
∮	Church or chapel with spire
+	Church or chapel without tower or spire
○	Chimney or tower
⊘	Glasshouse
+	Graticule intersection at 5' intervals
Ⓗ	Heliport
△	Triangulation pillar
⅄	Windmill with or without sails
⅄	Windpump

Boundaries

+ — + — +	National
–○–○–○–○–○–	London borough
	National park or forest park
NT	National Trust
—·—·—·—·—	County, region or islands area
–+–+–+–+–	District

NT open access
NT limited access

Abbreviations

P	Post office
PH	Public house
MS	Milestone
MP	Milepost
CH	Clubhouse
PC	Public convenience (in rural areas)
TH	Town hall, guildhall or equivalent
CG	Coastguard

Antiquities

VILLA	Roman
Castle	Non-Roman
⤬	Battlefield (with date)
☆	Tumulus
+	Position of antiquity which cannot be drawn to scale
𝔪	Ancient monuments and historic buildings in the care of the Secretaries of State for the Environment, for Scotland and for Wales and that are open to the public

Heights

—50—	Contours are at 10 metres vertical interval
·144	Heights are to the nearest metre above mean sea level

Heights shown close to a triangulation pillar refer to the station height at ground level and not necessarily to the summit

South from Princes Risborough through the Chilterns to Hambleden

The Chilterns provide some of the very best cycling close to London. Turning down yet another tiny lane in the midst of beechwoods, it is hard to imagine that the centre of London is only 48 km (30 miles) away. There are many pretty villages of brick and flint and a concentration of excellent pubs, even in the most unlikely places. This ride forms a cigar-shaped loop and runs roughly north-south from Princes Risborough up over Bledlow Ridge. It continues through glorious woodland down the Hambleden valley, passing the villages of Fingest and Skirmett, to Hambleden itself. A climb out of the valley, including one short but extra-ordinarily steep patch, brings you up to the ridge. It is worth diverting to visit West Wycombe village, with its collection of architectural styles and its church set amongst an old Iron Age fort. The busy A4010 is crossed near Saunderton and a last climb takes you past the windmill at Lacey Green, where the views from the escarpment edge are spectacular. A fast woodland descent takes you back to Princes Risborough.

Start

The library at the end of the High Street, Princes Risborough

P Follow signs from clock tower onto Church Street

Distance and grade

48 km (30 miles)

Moderate/strenuous

Terrain

Lots of short climbs and four main ones: 120 m (400 ft) from Princes Risborough onto Bledlow Ridge, 82 m (270 ft) up onto the next ridge, 120 m (400 ft) from Hambleden to Frieth and 91 m (300 ft) from the A4010 at Saunderton to Lacey Green

Nearest railway

Princes Risborough

Princes Risborough · Town End · The City · Waterend · Beacon's Bottom · Fingest · Skirmett · Hambleden

Fingest 10

Fingest is an attractive village of flint, brick and timber-framed buildings. St Bartholomews Church has an unusual tower.

Refreshments

The Crown PH, Bennett End
Studley Arms PH, Studley Green
Chequers Inn PH ❦❦, Fingest
Kings Arms PH ❦, *Old Crown PH* ❦❦,
Skirmett *Stag and Huntsman PH* ❦❦,
Hambleden *Old Sun PH* ❦ *and
others in* Lane End *Whip Inn PH*,
Loosley Row *Pink and Lily PH* ❦❦,
north of Lacey Green

Hambleden 12

Hambleden is one of the most attractive villages in the Chilterns. The clustered cottages date from the 16th century and the manor house is from the 17th century. Until 1956 the water pump at the centre of the village was the main water supply. In the churchyard is a memorial to William Henry Smith, who turned his family firm into Britain's leading newsagent.

West Wycombe Park 15/16

This Palladian house, with frescoes and painted ceilings, was fashioned in the mid-18th century for Sir Francis Dashwood, Chancellor of the Exchequer and founder of the infamous Hellfire Club. The landscaped gardens contain various temples.

West Wycombe Village and Hill 15/16

This Chiltern village has buildings from six centuries. The hill is part of the 18th-century landscaped gardens of West Wycombe Park and is surmounted by an Iron Age hillfort in which stand the church and Dashwood Mausoleum. There are fine views from the church tower and in it is a room seating ten people where members of the Hellfire Club are said to have practised black magic.

Lacey Green Windmill 19

Built in 1650, this is the third oldest smockmill in the country. It originally stood at Chesham and was only moved to Lacey Green in 1821. Once in a ruinous condition, it has now been fully restored by the Chiltern Society.

Parmoor   Frieth   Ditchfield   Wheeler End   West Wycombe   Saunderton Station   Lacey Green

1 With back to the library R on A4010 towards High Wycombe. After 800 m (½ mile), on sharp LH bend bear R onto Station Road (B4444) 'Bledlow 2, Chinnor 4'

2 As road turns sharp right L on Picts Lane 'Saunderton ½, Horsenden 1, Bledlow 2'

3 At T-j R onto Bledlow Road 'Horsenden, Bledlow 2, Chinnor 4' and over railway bridge

4 1st R onto Oddley Lane by a triangle of grass 'Bledlow 1½, Chinnor 3½'

5 At T-j at end of Oddley Lane L on Bledlow Ridge Road 'Bledlow Ridge 2, High Wycombe 8½'

6 Steep climb. At T-j at top of hill, by a triangle of grass R onto Chinnor Road 'Radnage 1, Chinnor 3, Stokenchurch 4', then 1st L onto Radnage Lane 'Radnage 2, Stokenchurch 4'

7 Ignore left and right turns and follow signs for Stokenchurch. 800 m (½ mile) after Crown PH on the right next L onto Foresters Road 'Waterend ¼, Beacon's Bottom ½, High Wycombe 6'

8 At T-j with A40, by triangle of grass and Studley Arms PH R 'Stokenchurch 1½', then 1st L 'Horsleys Green'

9 Cross M40. At T-j with B482 R 'Stokenchurch', then L on Chequers Lane

➡ **three pages**

15 Steep descent. At T-j with A40 R (NS). Use cycleway. 1st L 'Bledlow Ridge 3'

16 After 1 km (¾ mile) 1st R on Chorley Road 'Single track road with passing places'

17 At X-roads with A4010 SA onto Smalldean Lane

18 At X-roads at the end of Smalldean Lane L 'Lacey Green ½, Princes Risborough 3'

19 Short busy section. At X-roads by the Whip Inn PH R onto Pink Road 'Great Hampden 2½, Great Missenden 6'

20 Fine views to the left. At X-roads by Pink and Lily PH L on Wardrobes Lane 'Princes Risborough', then 1st R on Brimmers Road 'Princes Risborough ½, Aylesbury 10'

21 At roundabout L 'High Wycombe A4010' to return to start

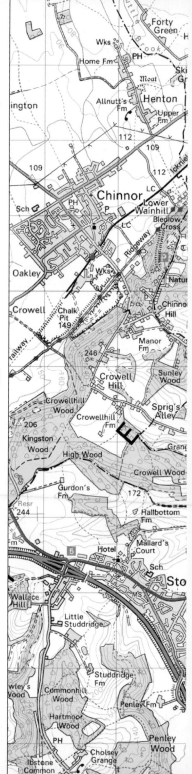

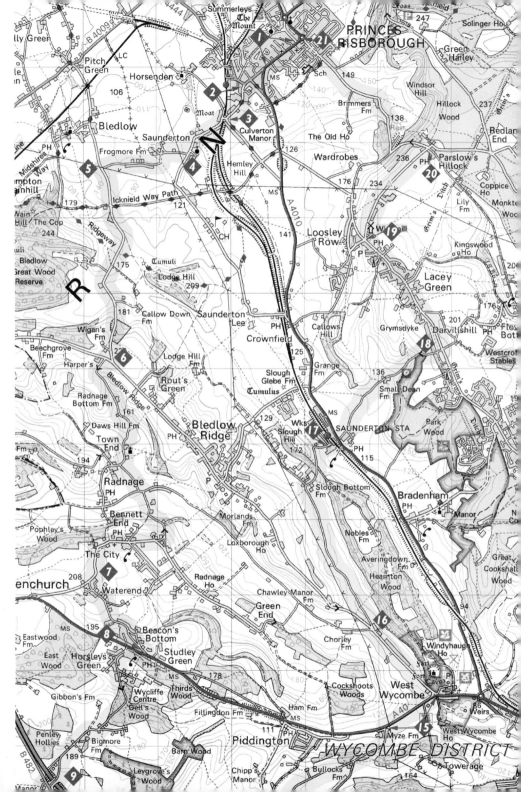

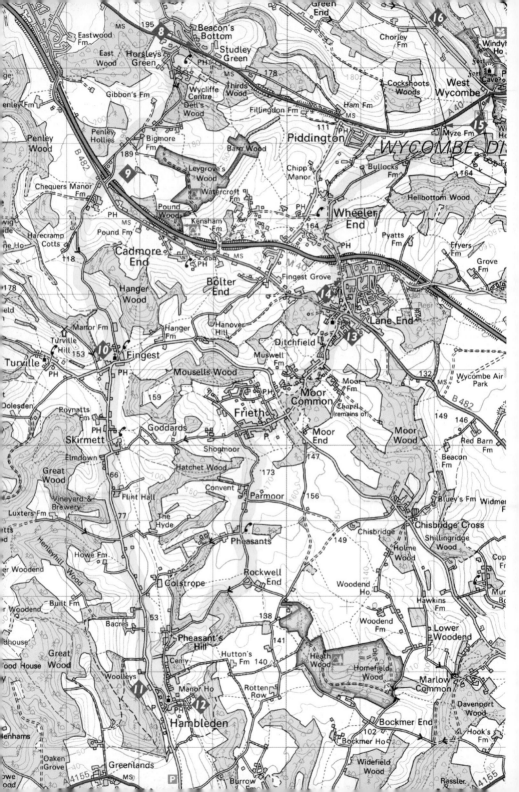

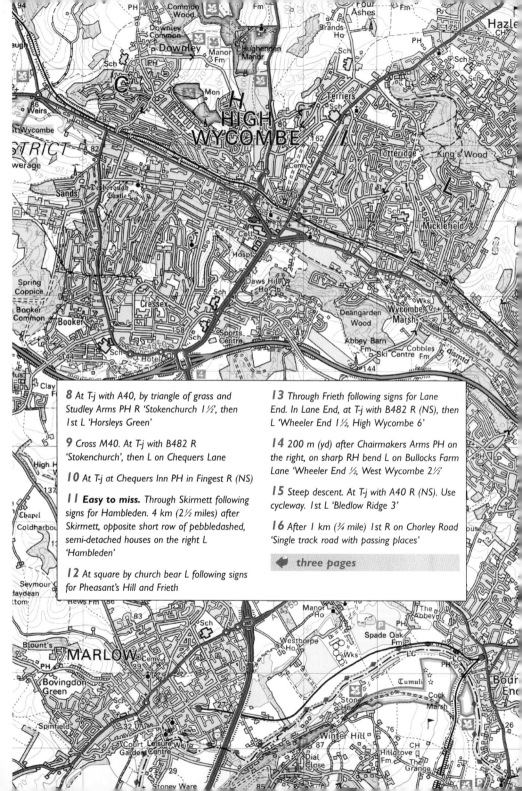

8 At T-j with A40, by triangle of grass and Studley Arms PH R 'Stokenchurch 1½', then 1st L 'Horsleys Green'

9 Cross M40. At T-j with B482 R 'Stokenchurch', then L on Chequers Lane

10 At T-j at Chequers Inn PH in Fingest R (NS)

11 Easy to miss. Through Skirmett following signs for Hambleden. 4 km (2½ miles) after Skirmett, opposite short row of pebbledashed, semi-detached houses on the right L 'Hambleden'

12 At square by church bear L following signs for Pheasant's Hill and Frieth

13 Through Frieth following signs for Lane End. In Lane End, at T-j with B482 R (NS), then L 'Wheeler End 1½, High Wycombe 6'

14 200 m (yd) after Chairmakers Arms PH on the right, on sharp RH bend L on Bullocks Farm Lane 'Wheeler End ½, West Wycombe 2½'

15 Steep descent. At T-j with A40 R (NS). Use cycleway. 1st L 'Bledlow Ridge 3'

16 After 1 km (¾ mile) 1st R on Chorley Road 'Single track road with passing places'

◀ three pages

2 *Through the Chilterns from Chesham to Tring*

On the map, Chesham appears to be at the centre of a spider's web with no fewer than 14 roads and lanes radiating out from the centre. At the start of the ride, you may well feel you have been sent on the wrong road as you exit from town on a busy road and then go through the industrial estate. However, after only a kilometre (¾ mile) from the start, you are into the countryside on a tiny, quiet lane that climbs 140 m (460 ft) through attractive farmland and beechwoods to one of the three high points of the ride at Hastoe, on the Ridgeway. You lose height rapidly as you dive down into Tring and the nearby nature reserves. The climb up from Tring is very steep, with a particularly tough section just before the top of the hill. Once back on the Chiltern escarpment, there is a roller coaster ride of six further climbs and descents, mostly through fine beechwoods, before finally swooping back down into Chesham.

Start

The Red Lion PH, in the centre of Chesham

P Follow signs

Distance and grade

48 km (30 miles)

Strenuous

Terrain

The first 137 m (450 ft) climb rises steadily over 10 km (6 miles) from the start to Hastoe. The climb up from Tring is the steepest, but there are six more of 30–91 m (100–300 ft). Lowest point – 100 m (330 ft) at Chesham. Highest point – 253 m (830 ft) on the Ridgeway north of Dunsmore

Nearest railway

Chesham. Alternatively Tring, Wendover or Great Missenden are all near to the route

Chesham   Cholesbury   Tring   Lee Gate

Places of interest

Chesham 1
The George Inn, in the pedestrian-ised High Street, dates from 1715. A charter granted in 1257 by King Henry III gave Chesham its market, held every Wednesday

Cholesbury 4
Cholesbury Common boasts of a fine tower windmill that started life as a smock mill in 1863 and has now been converted into a private house

Tring 8
Tring Reservoirs National Reserve is home to many water birds including great crested grebe, heron and pochard

 ## Refreshments

Queens Head PH 🍵, plenty of choice in **Chesham**
Blue Ball PH 🍵, **Asheridge**
Full Moon PH, **Cholesbury**
Plenty of choice in **Tring**
Old Swan PH, The Gate PH, **Lee Gate** Fox PH 🍵, **Dunsmore**
Hampden Arms PH 🍵, **Hampden**
The Gate PH 🍵, **Bryant's Bottom**
Bat and Ball PH, **Holmer Green**
Red Lion PH 🍵, Crown PH 🍵, **Little Missenden**

Dunsmore

Great Hampden

Great Kingshill

I **Take care** on the busy section to exit Chesham. With back to the Red Lion PH in the centre of Chesham L. At 1st roundabout R 'Berkhamsted A416'. At next roundabout SA 'Berkhamsted A416' then 1st L 'Bellington 2½'

2 Shortly after passing Griffin PH L onto Asheridge Road 'Asheridge Industrial Estate'. Follow this lane for 5 km (3 miles)

➡ **two pages**

16 **Ignore** the 1st right which turns sharply back on itself. Take the next R shortly after old brick and timber farm to the left 'Great Hampden 1, Speen 2½, Wycombe 7'

17 At X-roads at top of hill R 'Great Hampden, Speen 2, Princes Risbrough 4'

18 Immediately after Hampden arms PH in Great Hampden L 'Bryant's Bottom 1¼, High Wycombe 5¾'

19 Follow signs for Brayant's Bottom. At T-j at bottom of the hill L (NS)

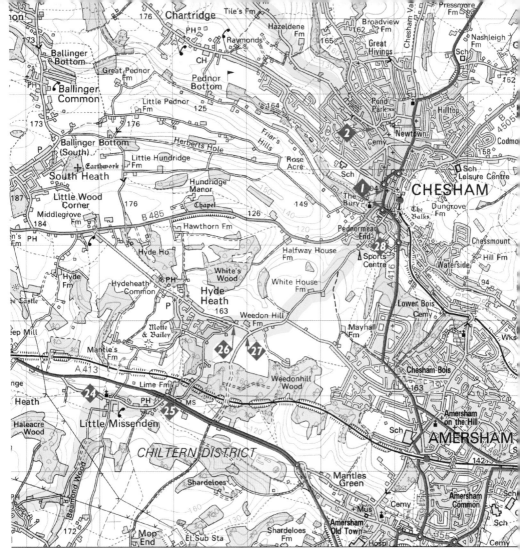

20 At X-roads with Hampden Road SA onto Hatches Lane 'Great Kingshill I'

21 At T-j in Great Kingshill at the end of Hatches Lane L then R onto The Common. Shortly at next T-j, with red brick houses ahead, R (NS)

22 At T-j at the end of Copes Road R

23 At double mini-roundabout by petrol station SA onto Beech Tree Road. (Busy section). Continue in same direction following signs for Little Missenden past the Bat and Ball PH

24 AT T-j in Little Missenden R 'Amersham'

25 At X-roads with A413 SA (NS). The lane/layby swings R then L up keepers Lane

26 At T-j at the end of Keepers Land bear R

27 At T-j at the end of continuation of keepers Lane L (NS). (There is a sign for Hyde Heath to the left). Follow signs for Chesham up and down Fullers Hill

28 At T-j at the bottom of hill bear R (in effect SA) onto Germain Street to return to start

2 Shortly after passing Griffin PH L onto Asheridge Road 'Asheridge Industrial Estate'. Follow this lane for 5 km (3 miles)

3 At T-j L 'Cholesbury 1, St Leonards 2' then shortly bear R by triangle of grass and pond onto Rays Hill (**Or** for short cut avoiding Tring bear L at triangle of grass, follow road for 3 km (2 miles) into St Leonards and rejoin route at instruction 12)

4 At T-j at top of Rays Hill L then shortly 1st R 'Wigginton 2, Tring 3'

5 After 400 m (¼ mile) 1st L onto Shire Lane

6 After 4 km (2½ miles), at bottom of hill, at T-j with Hastoe Lane L 'Tring ¾'

7 At T-j with Park Road at the end of Hastoe Lane R

8 At T-j with High Street L

9 Go past the Anchor PH (on your left). Shortly after passing a car dealer on your right take the 2nd L by telephone box onto Duckmore Lane. Go under the A41

10 At triangle of grass bear R (in effect SA) (NS). Very steep, wooded climb. Gentle descent

11 Easy to miss. 1 km (¾ mile) after passing the mast at the top of the wooded climb 1st R by triangle of grass onto Gilberts Hill (NS)

12 At T-j at the end of Gilberts Hill R 'Wendover' then L (NS)

13 At X-roads shortly after the Old Swan PH R 'Kingsash 1, Wendover 3½'. Steep descent

14 At T-j with A413 L 'Great Missenden' then R 'Dunsmore 1'. Steep climb. Follow signs for Kimble and Princes Risborough

15 Steep descent. At T-j by triangle of grass L 'Great Hampden 3, Great Missenden 5'

16 Ignore the 1st right which turns sharply back on itself. Take the next R shortly after old brick and timber farm to the left 'Great Hampden 1, Speen 2½, Wycombe 7'

⬅ two pages

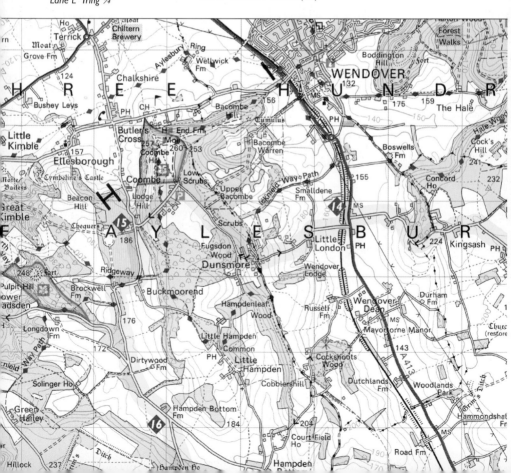

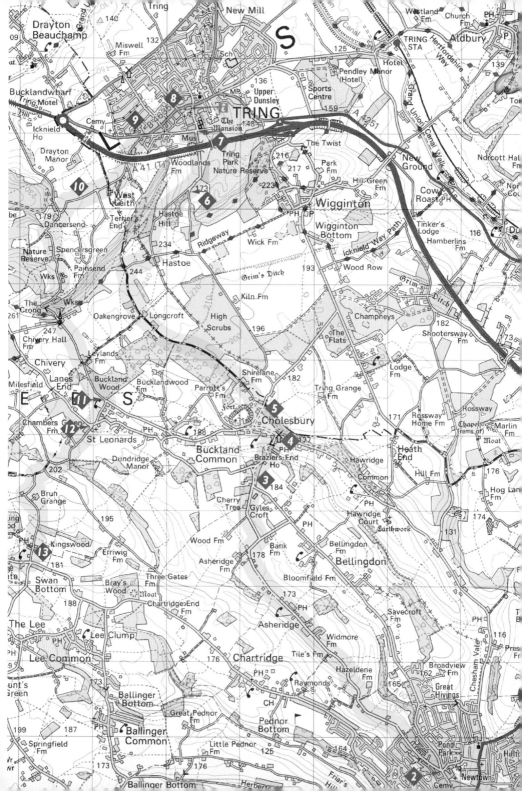

3 South from Royston over rolling downland to Buntingford

The downlands south of Royston are the highest point east of the Chilterns, rising to a summit of 168 m (553 ft) at Therfield. From Royston, you climb southwards through the pretty village of Barkway, with its half-timbered houses, before heading further west to Buntingford. The High Street of this attractive town must have been a nightmare before the by-pass was built, but it is now possible to appreciate its former glory as a staging post on the A10 north from London. From Buntingford, the ride explores little-used lanes in fine, arable farmland, passing through the oddly named hamlet, Nasty. Finally, after turning northwards, visiting Ardeley, you come to the steep climb up to dizzying heights at Therfield, finishing with a fast descent back to Royston.

Start

The traffic lights in the centre of Royston near the Coach & Horses PH

P Follow Melbourn Road (A10 towards Cambridge). At roundabout L onto King James Way and long-stay car park

Distance and grade

50 km (31 miles)

Moderate

Terrain

Two climbs at the start of 51 m (170 ft) then 82 m (270 ft) to reach the mast near Barkway. Steady 70 m (230 ft) climb near the end of the ride, from south of Rushden to Therfield. Most of the ride undulates at 91–152 m (300-500 ft). Lowest point – 82 m (270 ft) at crossing of River Rib in Buntingford. Highest point – 168 m (553 ft) at Therfield

Barkway

Barkway

Buntingford

Great Munden

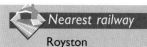

Nearest railway

Royston

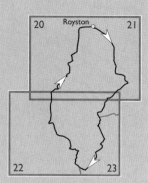

Refreshments

Coach & Horses PH 🍺, plenty of choice in **Royston**
Tally Ho PH, **Barkway**
Plenty of choice in **Buntingford**
Sword in Hand PH 🍺🍺, **Westmill**
Plough Inn, **Great Munden**
Rest & Welcome PH, **Haultwick**
Jolly Waggoner PH 🍺🍺, **Ardeley**
Moon & Stars PH 🍺🍺, **Rushden**
Chequers Inn, **Sandon**
Fox & Duck PH, **Therfield**

Places of interest

Royston Cave 1
A unique, bell-shaped chamber of unknown origin, cut from the chalk beneath Melbourn Street. The carvings are clearly medieval and most have religious and historical significance. It is believed to have been used by the Knights Templar before their proscription by the Pope in the 14th century (open in the afternoon on summer weekends)

Barkway 7
Attractive village of thatched cottages dating back to the 17th century. The village grew and prospered as a handy stopping place between Ware and Cambridge. The two tall milestones are part of what was probably the first example of regular milestone placing in Britain. In 1586, William Mowse, Master of Trinity Hall, Cambridge, left £1000 in his will to mend the highways in and around Cambridge and towards Barkway. A later Master, William Warren set up milestones along the whole length of the road between Cambridge and Barkway

▲ Barkway milestone

Wood End   Cromer   Kelshall

1 From the traffic lights, wheel your bike over the pavement and bear to the R of the bank onto the one way street

2 At T-j by the Chequers Hotel L and get into RH lane 'London A10, Barley B1309'

3 Follow the one-way system round, moving into the LH lane and following signs for Barley and Barkway. Steep climb. Start descending

4 On sharp LH bend 800 m (½ mile) after the brow of the hill turn R 'Newsells, Barkway'. Descend, then climb

5 At T-j by mast L 'Barkway, Hare Street'

6 At T-j with B1368 (Cambridge Road) by memorial cross R 'Hare Street, Braughing'

7 Through Barkway. At the end of the village, shortly after Tally Ho PH, L onto Nuthampstead Road 'Nuthampstead 2, Anstey 2, Meesden 4'

8 After 2 km (1¼ miles) 1st R 'Anstey'

9 After 2 km (1¼ miles) 1st R 'Wyddial, Buntingford'

10 At X-roads with B1368 SA 'Wyddial'

➡ **two pages**

22 1 km (¾ mile) after Moon & Stars PH in Rushden 1st R (shortly after the drive to 'Julians') 'Sandon, Kelshall'

23 At T-j by the telephone box in Roe Green R 'Sandon ¾, Kelshall 2¼, Buckland 3¼'

24 Go past the Chequers Inn. Immediately after pond on the right next L towards church 'Kelshall, Therfield, Royston' then shortly 1st R (same sign)

25 At T-j R 'Therfield, Royston'

26 At T-j L 'Royston 3'

27 At T-j at the bottom of hill R 'Royston Town Centre' to return to the start

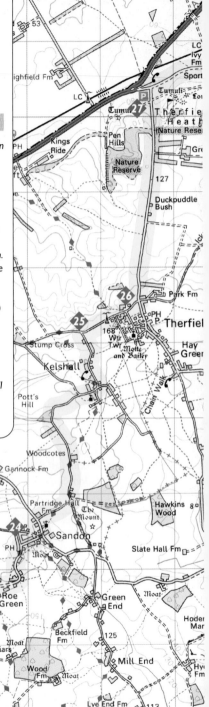

11 After 5½ km (3½ miles), at the roundabout at the start of Buntingford, L onto Ermine Street

12 At T-j, at the end of the High Street by the Black Bull PH, bear L (in effect SA)

13 Go past the Jolly Sailor PH and the Fire Station. At the Railway PH R onto Aspenden Road 'Aspenden ½, Westmill 1¼'

14 Under the main road and 1st L (NS). Follow this road for 7 km (4½ miles) passing through Westmill, Nasty and Great Munden

15 Shortly after passing Plough Inn PH ignore the first right (the drive to Libury Hall). Take the next R by triangle of grass 'Haultwick ½'

16 At T-j by triangle of grass in Haultwick by the Rest and Welcome PH R 'Wood End, Ardeley'

17 At T-j by triangle of grass L 'Ardeley'

18 At The Jolly Waggoner PH in Ardeley R 'Cottered'

19 After 1 km (¾ mile) 1st L 'Cromer' then shortly, at T-j with B1037 L 'Walkern'

20 After 600 m (yd) on sharp LH bend 1st R 'Baldock'

21 At T-j with A507 bear L (in effect SA) 'Baldock' then follow signs 'Local Traffic, Rushden'

22 1 km (¾ mile) after Moon & Stars PH in Rushden 1st R (shortly after the drive to 'Julians') 'Sandon, Kelshall'

◀ **two pages**

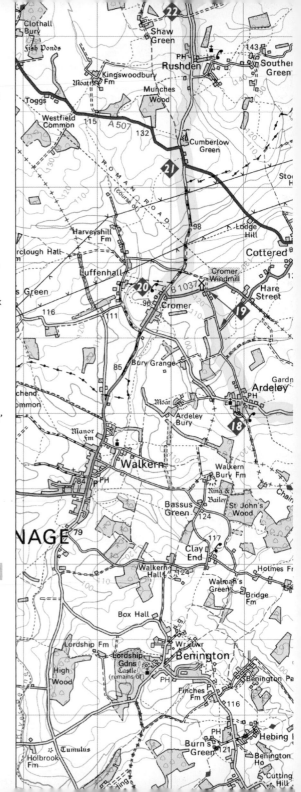

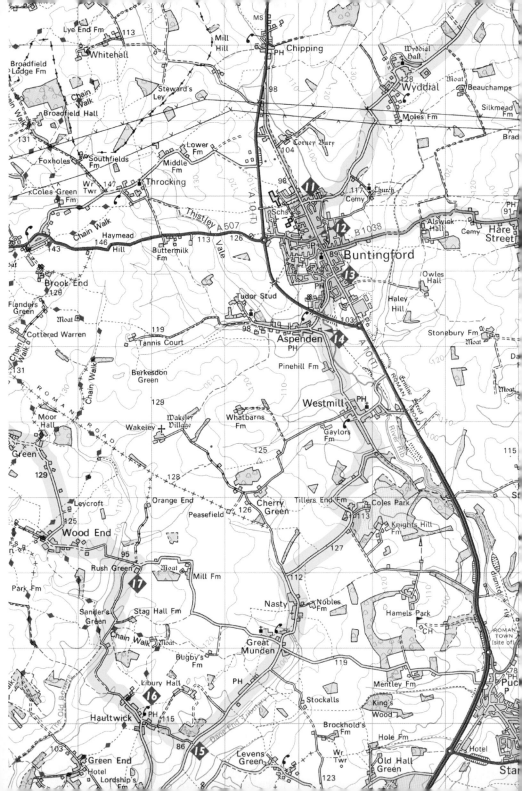

4 West from Stansted Mountfitchet to Buntingford

With the exception of two short stretches, through Much Hadham and near Buntingford, the whole course of this easy route is on quiet lanes, which is something of a surprise given its proximity to so many centres of population. There are several good pubs along the way. The highlights include the crossing of Barwick ford close to the A10, the village and pub at Westmill and the attractive town of Buntingford.

▼ The High Street, Much Hadham

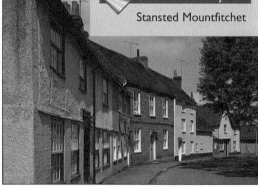

Stansted Mountfitchet 1

A busy town with a motte-and-bailey castle built in Norman times. It was destroyed by King John and has now been recreated and displays a giant catapult, a thatched falconry and the white-washed Grand Hall with a row of well-preserved 16th-century houses below

Much Hadham 7

Showpiece village, for centuries the country seat of the Bishops of London. Their palace, near the 12th-century church, is mainly Jacobean. The main street has a mixture of Elizabethan cottages and Regency houses

Westmill 11

Near to this pretty village, complete with green and tall-chimneyed cottages surrounding the church, stands a cottage bought by the 19th-century essayist Charles Lamb. This thatched, 17th-century cottage with the evocative name of Button Snap is now owned by the Lamb Society

Furneux Pelham 15

The largest of the three Pelham villages owned in Norman times by the de Furneux family. The gloriously restored 15th-century church has windows by Morris and Burne-Jones. There is also a brewery and an adjacent pub – The Brewery Tap

Manuden 17

Facing the churchyard gate to The Street, a sagging house with a wavy roof and similarly undulating timbers along its overhanging upper storey was built in the 14th century, then rebuilt in Elizabethan times. Manuden House, a Queen Anne mansion with a 19th-century stucco coating, stands on a bend in The Street behind impressive iron railings with gilded owls peering down from the gates

Refreshments

Plenty of choice in **Stansted Mountfitchet**
Three Horseshoes PH, **Hazel End**
Nags Head PH ❦**, Little Hadham**
Jolly Waggoners PH ❦**, Bull PH** ❦**, plenty of choice in* **Much Hadham**
Duke of Wellington PH, **Barwick**
Plough PH, **Great Munden**
Sword in Hand PH ❦❦**, Westmill**
Lots of choice in **Buntingford**
Star PH, Brewery Tap PH, **Furneux Pelham**

Nasty   Buntingford   Hare Street   Furneux Pelham

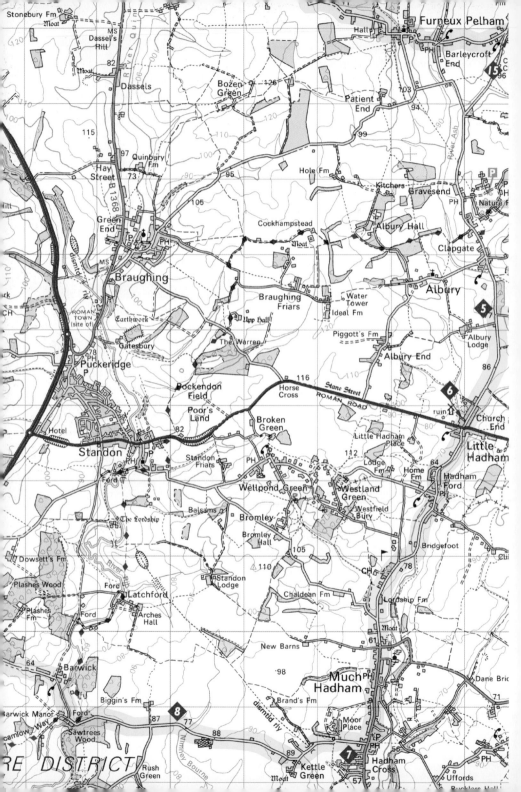

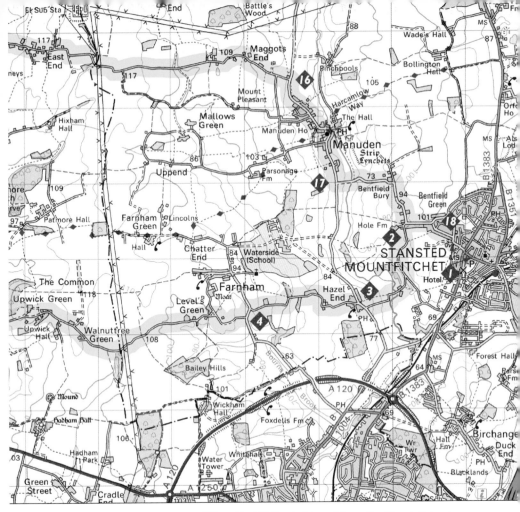

1 With back to the Library R. At X-roads with B1383 SA onto Bentfield Road. Shortly after sharp RH bend and just past a thatched cottage on the left L 'Manuden'

2 Shortly after last houses at the edge of the town, on sharp RH bend with triangle of grass bear L 'Hazel End'. After 1 km (¾ mile) bear R by white railings (NS)

3 At T-j by Three Horseshoes PH R then L 'Farnham'

4 At T-j L sharply back on yourself then 1st R by triangle of grass 'Albury, Upwick'. Shortly 1st L (same sign)

5 At T-j L 'The Hadhams'

6 At traffic lights with A120 in Little Hadham R then L 'Golf Course 2'

7 At far end of Much Hadham, shortly after Old Crown PH, next R onto Kettle Green Road

8 Follow signs for Barwick Ford then Dane End for 6½ km (4 miles)

➡ **next page**

15 At offset X-roads R then L 'East End, Manuden'

16 At T-j R 'Manuden'. Through Manuden

17 Shortly after last houses 1st L 'Stansted, Elsenham'. Follow signs for Stansted

18 At T-j with red brick house ahead R onto Bentfield Road. At X-roads with B1383 SA to return to start

9 Take care – busy road. At T-j with A10 L 'London' (use pavement) then 1st R 'Standon Green End, Whitehill Golf Centre'. Follow signs for Dane End and The Mundens to the bottom of a long hill

10 At T-j R 'Great Munden'

11 Follow this road for 8 km (5 miles) through Great Munden, Nasty and Westmill. At T-j in Aspenden by triangle of grass with a tree R 'Buntingford'

12 At T-j with Station Road in Buntingford L then 2nd R by the Jolly Sailor PH onto Hare Street Road 'B1038. Hare Street, Brent Pelham'

13 At T-j (with B1368) R 'Braughing, Puckeridge' then 1st L 'Furneux Pelham'

14 After 1 km (¾ mile) 1st R 'Little Hormead, Furneux Pelham'. Through Furneux Pelham following signs for Manuden

15 At offset X-roads R then L 'East End, Manuden'

◀ *previous page*

Buntingford

B1038

126

Tudor Stud

Haley Hill

98

12

11

Aspenden

PH

Pinehill Fm

Westmill

PH

Whatbarns Fm

Gaylors Fm

125

Ermine Street Roman Road

River Rib

Fm

St John's Wood

Chain Walk

Leycroft

Orange End

Peasefield

126

Cherry Green

Tillers End Fm

Coles Park

113

125

Wood End

Parker's Green

95

Rush Green

Moat

Mill Fm

127

Knights Fm

Holmes Fm

Walkern Park Fm

Bridge Fm

Sander's Green

Stag Hall Fm

Chain Walk

Moat

112

Nasty

Nobles Fm

Hamels

Bugby's Fm

Great Munden

110

Benington Park

Chain Walk

Libury Hall

PH

119

Mentley Fm

116

Haultwick

PH

115

Stockalls

King's Wood

Hebing End

103

Green End

Hotel

Lordship's Fm

86

The Old Bourne

Dane End Tributary

Levens Green

Brockhold's Fm

Hole Fm

Wr Twr

123

Old Hall Green

Benington Ho

Cutting Hill

Chain Walk

Comb's Wood

High Trees Fm

College

Chapel Fm

Dane End

P

10

PH

Moorfield Common

Whitehill Fm

117

CH

Hill Fm

Roman Road

18

102

68

Whempstead

8

Brookfield Common

Smart's Hill

Lodge Fm

Rigery Fm

111

Collier End

PH

108

Bromley Common

Chain Walk

90

Rowney Priory

99

Potter's Green

Labdens Fm

105

Sacombe Hill Fm

62

112

Sacombe Green

ROMAN ROAD

Standon Green End

9

Bardolphs

ROMAN

Sacombe

West from Writtle along quiet lanes and through the Rodings

Start

The Inn on the Green, Writtle, west of Chelmsford

P Car park off the green

Distance and grade

45 km (28 miles)

Easy

Terrain

Very gently undulating countryside. No hills. Lowest point – 30 m (100 ft) in Writtle. Highest point – 80 m (265 ft) at several points

Nearest railway

Chelmsford 2 km (1¼ miles) east of the start. Chipping Ongar, 3 km (2 miles) south of the route at Fyfield

The first 3 km (2 miles) of this ride give no indication of the delights that are in store beyond the outskirts of Chelmsford. 1 km (¾ mile) of the busy A1060 and a section of Chelmsford's leafy suburbs form a total contrast to the quiet Essex lanes that lead westwards to the Rodings. For a ride that picks its way among the region's network of country lanes, it comes as a pleasant surprise that you follow the same lane for 11 km (7 miles) without turning off to right or left, from the outskirts of Chelmsford to High Easter where there is a fine pub. The ride continues southwards through rich agricultural country to Fyfield, beyond which it becomes slightly more fractured as it twists and turns its way back to the large green in Writtle.

34 35

32 33

Chelmsford

Writtle

Chignall St James

High Easter

Writtle 1

The central green of Writtle slopes gently towards its pond that originally supplied water for traction engines. All around the green are houses of different styles, from the Tudor-timbered splendour of Aubyns, near the church, through elegant Georgian brickwork, to varieties of pargeted plaster. Some of the pargeting has quite sizable relief bosses. The nearby 162 ha (400 acre) Hylands Park has woods and lakes

Refreshments

Plenty of choice in **Writtle**
Three Elms PH, **Chignall St James**
Fox PH a, north of **Mashbury**
Cork & Bell Inn 🍴🍺, Punchbowl PH,
High Easter
(White Horse PH 🍴🍺, **Pleshey,**
just off the route)
Axe & Compass PH 🍺,
Aythorpe Roding
Black Horse PH 🍺, **White Roding**
Black Bull PH 🍴🍺,
Queens Head PH, **Fyfield**
Maltsters Arms PH, **Willingale**

Pleshey 5 (just off the route)

Ancient Britons settled the site, hacking out a 16 ha (40 acre) enclosure; the Romans displaced them and added their own entrenchments; and the Saxons called it Tumblestoun from the ancient mounds that were left. The Normans in turn took over: today, the village, encircled by the massive Norman earthworks that formed their castle bailey, is most picturesque. A short walk to the castle mound over the amazing 15th-century, single-span, brick bridge is rewarded with fine views

The Rodings 7/11

Eight villages and hamlets (Abbess, Aythorpe, Beauchamp, Berners, High, Leaden, Margaret and White Roding) strung along the valley of the River Roding. Most are picturesque with old churches, moated halls, half-timbered cottages and comfortable pubs

Abbess Roding   Little Laver   Fyfield   Radley Green   Great Oxney Green

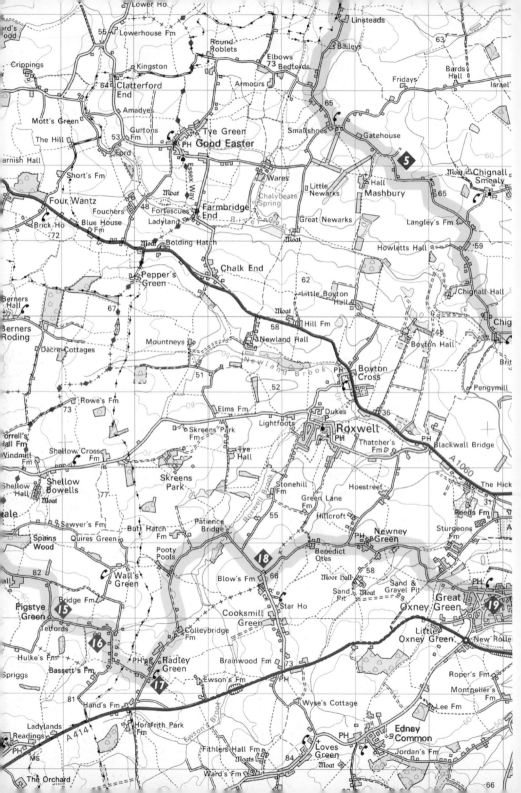

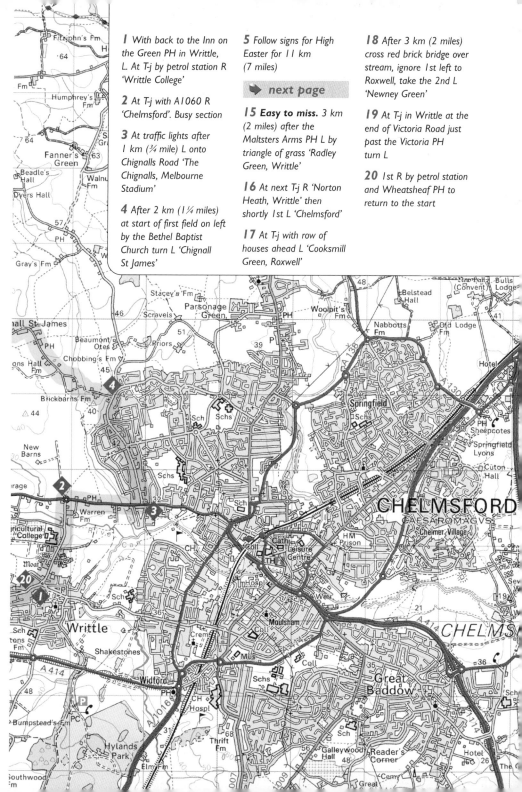

1 With back to the Inn on the Green PH in Writtle, L. At T-j by petrol station R 'Writtle College'

2 At T-j with A1060 R 'Chelmsford'. Busy section

3 At traffic lights after 1 km (¾ mile) L onto Chignalls Road 'The Chignalls, Melbourne Stadium'

4 After 2 km (1¼ miles) at start of first field on left by the Bethel Baptist Church turn L 'Chignall St James'

5 Follow signs for High Easter for 11 km (7 miles)

➤ next page

15 *Easy to miss.* 3 km (2 miles) after the Maltsters Arms PH L by triangle of grass 'Radley Green, Writtle'

16 At next T-j R 'Norton Heath, Writtle' then shortly 1st L 'Chelmsford'

17 At T-j with row of houses ahead L 'Cooksmill Green, Roxwell'

18 After 3 km (2 miles) cross red brick bridge over stream, ignore 1st left to Roxwell, take the 2nd L 'Newney Green'

19 At T-j in Writtle at the end of Victoria Road just past the Victoria PH turn L

20 1st R by petrol station and Wheatsheaf PH to return to the start

6 *400 m (yd) after the pubs in High Easter, on sharp LH bend with barns to the right, turn R (NS)*

7 *At triangle of grass by Hill Farm bear L 'Aythorpe Roding'*

8 *At X-roads with B184 by the Axe & Compass PH SA 'Aythorpe Roding Church'*

9 *After 4 km (2½ miles) at T-j with triangle of grass R 'White Roding ¾, Sawbridgeworth Station 6, Bishops Stortford 8'. At main road R*

10 *After 1 km (¾ mile) on this busy road 1st L by Black Horse PH 'Abbess Roding 2, Matching Green 3'*

11 *At T-j by triangle of grass R 'Fyfield, Ongar'. Follow signs for Little Laver through Abbess Roding*

12 **Easy to miss.** *After 4 km (2½ miles) and shortly after telephone box in Little Laver 1st L by triangle of grass 'Moreton, Ongar'*

13 *At T-j by triangle of grass L 'Fyfield, Ongar'*

14 *At T-j with B184 L 'Dunmow 12' then, by the Queens Head PH R 'Church, Willingale'. Follow signs for Writtle*

15 **Easy to miss.** *3 km (2 miles) after the Maltsters Arms PH L by triangle of grass 'Radley Green, Writtle'*

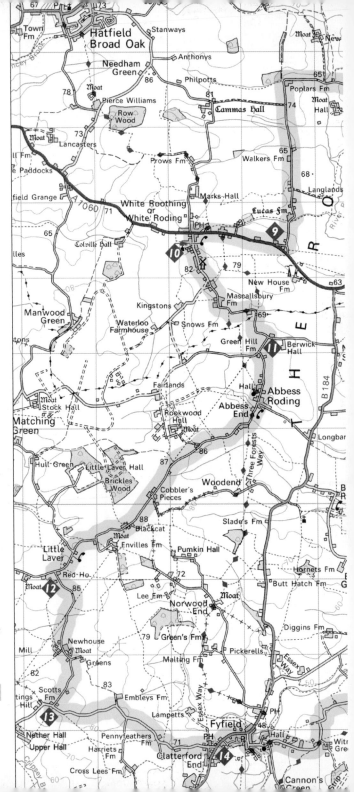

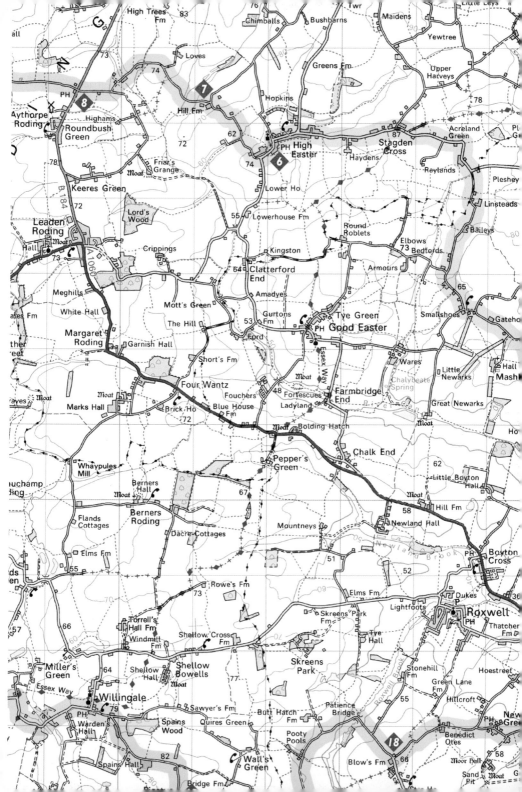

6 *South from Coggeshall to the Blackwater Estuary at Tollesbury*

Coggeshall is one of Essex's most attractive villages with many fine old houses along its streets. The ride heads east on quiet lanes towards Colchester before turning south and passing beneath the busy A12. South from Copford, there are occasionally views down to the Blackwater Estuary, one of the three major estuaries in East Anglia, north of the Thames. The penultimate section, through Kelvedon and Feering, is the least appealing part of the ride but after leaving Feering, 3 km (2 miles) of lanes, parallel with the River Blackwater, bring you back to the delights of Coggeshall.

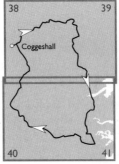

 Start

The clocktower in Coggeshall, west of Colchester

P Car park on the street beyond the clocktower

 **Distance and grade**

51 km (32 miles)

Easy

Terrain

No major hills. Lowest point – sea level at Tollesbury. Highest point – 76 m (250 ft) at Great Braxted

 Nearest railway

Kelvedon, on the route

Refreshments

Fleece PH 🍴🍴, plenty of choice in **Coggeshall**
Chequers PH, **Great Tey**
Swan PH, **Copford**
Alma PH, **Copford Green**
Hare & Hounds PH, **Birch Green**
Hope PH, **Tollesbury**
Red Lion PH, **Tolleshunt D'Arcy**
Du Cane Arms PH, **Great Braxted**
Plenty of choice in **Kelvedon**

 Great Tey   Aldham   Copford   Birch Green

Coggeshall 1

Medieval village noted for merchants' houses with fine woodcarving. The best example is Paycocke's House, dating from 1500, which houses a display of lace. Coggeshall Abbey was founded in 1140 by King Stephen, then taken over by Cistercian monks, who learnt the art of brick-making from sister houses on the continent and thus re-established brick manufacture in England for the first time since the departure of the Romans

▲ Coggeshall Abbey

The Layers 12/13

Two 'Layer' villages and one hamlet: Layer Breton with remote church set in heath; Layer-de-la-Haye where you can see the wildfowl of Abberton Reservoir and Layer Marney with a red-brick gatehouse – the only completed part of a 16th-century mansion that is decorated with terracotta shells and dolphins

Abberton Reservoir 12/13

Popular nature reserve for winter wildlife, particularly ducks. Osprey visit in spring and autumn

Tollesbury 16

The 18th-century font in St Mary's church bears the inscription 'Good people all I pray take care, that in ye church you do not sware. As this man did'. The font was paid for by a drunken man who swore in the church and was persuaded to make the donation to avoid prosecution. Tollesbury once had a fishing fleet and at the turn of the century more than 100 sailing smacks brought in their catches of sprats for pickling

Tollesbury   Tolleshunt D'Arcy   Great Totham   Kelvedon

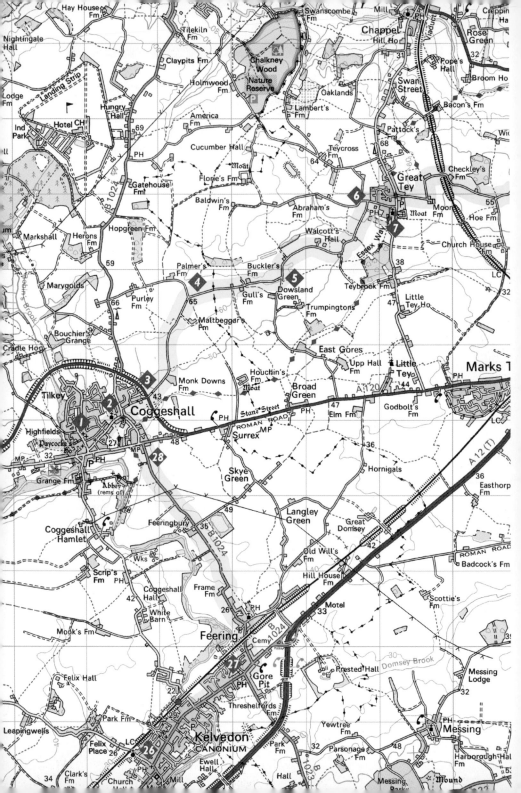

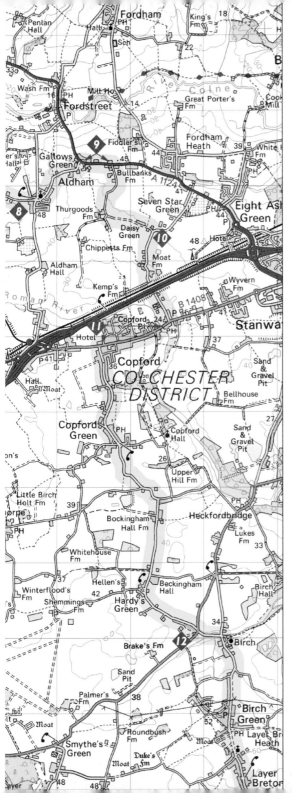

1 From the clocktower, Coggeshall take the road signposted 'Earls Colne' towards the church

2 At roundabout just past the church L onto Colne Road 'Earls Colne'. Shortly 1st R by Alexandra PH onto Tey Road 'No Through Road'

3 At X-roads with main road (A120) SA (NS)

4 At fork after 2 km (1¼ miles) bear R 'The Teys'

5 At T-j by triangle of grass L 'Great Tey'

6 At T-j on the edge of Great Tey by triangle of grass R 'Colchester'

7 At T-j by church at the end of The Street L onto Chappel Road '(A604) Chappel' then 1st R onto Moor Road 'Aldham'

8 At X-roads in Aldham SA onto Green Lane

9 At T-j with A604 R 'Colchester' then 1st R onto Foxes Lane (**take care**)

10 At T-j by triangle of grass R 'Stanway, Copford'

11 At T-j (with B1408) R then after 1 km (¾ mile), at the end of Copford, opposite petrol station L onto School Road 'Copford Green, Easthorpe, Birch'

12 After 5 km (3 miles) at X-roads with B1022 SA 'Birch 1, Layer Breton 2' (**take care**) then shortly, at T-j R 'Layer Breton, Great Wigborough, Tolleshunt D'Arcy'

➡ **next page**

26 At T-j at the end of Maldon Road bear R (in effect SA) 'Colchester'

27 Through Kelvedon. Cross the bridge over the River Blackwater and go through Feering. Shortly after right turn to Tiptree on the B1023 next L opposite car dealer 'Feering Village ¼'

28 At T-j by triangle of grass at the start of Coggeshall L then R onto St Peters Road. At roundabout L to return to the start

39

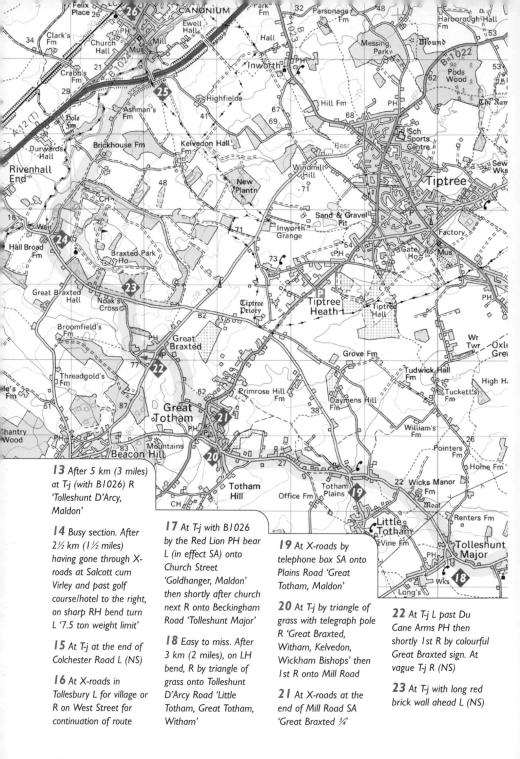

13 After 5 km (3 miles) at T-j (with B1026) R 'Tolleshunt D'Arcy, Maldon'

14 Busy section. After 2½ km (1½ miles) having gone through X-roads at Salcott cum Virley and past golf course/hotel to the right, on sharp RH bend turn L '7.5 ton weight limit'

15 At T-j at the end of Colchester Road L (NS)

16 At X-roads in Tollesbury L for village or R on West Street for continuation of route

17 At T-j with B1026 by the Red Lion PH bear L (in effect SA) onto Church Street 'Goldhanger, Maldon' then shortly after church next R onto Beckingham Road 'Tolleshunt Major'

18 Easy to miss. After 3 km (2 miles), on LH bend, R by triangle of grass onto Tolleshunt D'Arcy Road 'Little Totham, Great Totham, Witham'

19 At X-roads by telephone box SA onto Plains Road 'Great Totham, Maldon'

20 At T-j by triangle of grass with telegraph pole R 'Great Braxted, Witham, Kelvedon, Wickham Bishops' then 1st R onto Mill Road

21 At X-roads at the end of Mill Road SA 'Great Braxted ¾'

22 At T-j L past Du Cane Arms PH then shortly 1st R by colourful Great Braxted sign. At vague T-j R (NS)

23 At T-j with long red brick wall ahead L (NS)

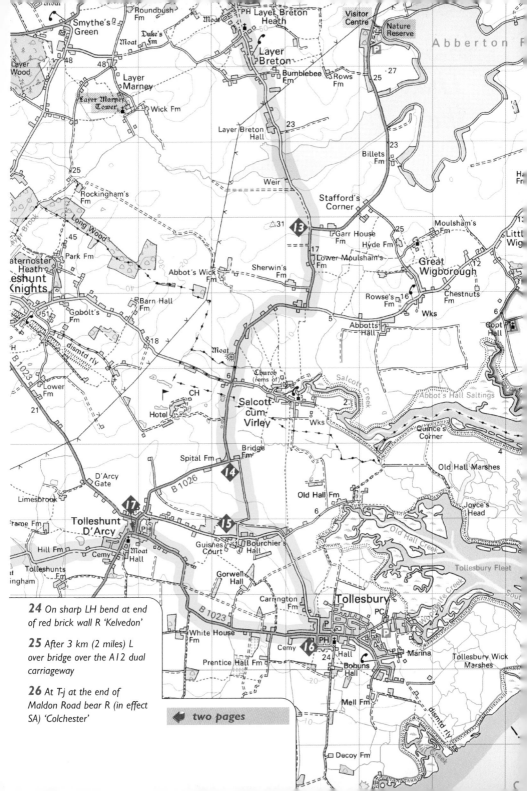

24 On sharp LH bend at end of red brick wall R 'Kelvedon'

25 After 3 km (2 miles) L over bridge over the A12 dual carriageway

26 At T-j at the end of Maldon Road bear R (in effect SA) 'Colchester'

⬅ **two pages**

South from Thaxted through the heart of Essex

Thaxted is one of Essex's most attractive villages with a large square boasting the very fine half-timbered Guildhall. The ride heads south along the valley of the River Chelmer from which Chelmsford derives its name. Great Dunmow is the one town encountered en route and could easily be used as an alternative starting point. The straight roads leading to and from the town give an indication of the Roman settlements that abounded in this area north of London. Fine pubs are passed at High Easter and Pleshey before the route turns north through Felsted, Little Dunmow and Stebbing on its way back to a well-earned tea stop in Thaxted.

 Start

The Guildhall, Thaxted, 16 km (10 miles) northeast of Bishop's Stortford

P Long-stay car park on Town Street at the bottom of the square in Thaxted

 Distance and grade

52 km (33 miles)

Easy

 Terrain

No real hills. Lowest point – 39 m (130 ft) the River Chelmer south of Felsted. Highest point – 100 m (340 ft) northwest of Lindsell

 Nearest railway

Braintree, 11 km (7 miles) east of the route at Stebbing

Thaxted

Little Easton

Great Dunmow

High Easter

Little Dunmow *(just off the route)* 5
The Dunmow Flitch trial is held here every four years to find a man and his wife who have not had a domestic brawl or wished to be unmarried for 12 months and a day. A flitch of bacon is presented to the couple able to prove this enviable state of affairs! The records of the awarding of the flitch in the 18th century are hung on the church walls

The Rodings 9
Eight villages and hamlets bear the name: Abbess, Aythorpe, Beauchamp, Berners, High, Leaden, Margaret and White Roding

Pleshey 13
Ancient Britons settled the site, hacking out a 40 acre enclosure; the Romans displaced them and added their own entrenchments; and the Saxons called it Tumblestoun from the ancient mounds that were left. The Normans in turn took over: today, the village, encircled by the massive Norman earthworks that formed their castle bailey, is most picturesque. A short walk to the castle mound over the amazing 15th-century, single-span, brick bridge is rewarded with fine views

Stebbing 17
Well-preserved buildings date from the Middle Ages and a handsome 18th-century water mill straddles the brook. The Great Mount earthwork is the site of a castle built by Richard De Vark in 1086. The moated Porter's Hall on Stebbing Green is an early 17th-century farmhouse

Refreshments

Plenty of choice, Swan PH 🍺, Star PH 🍺, **Thaxted**
The Stag PH, **Little Easton**
Green Man PH 🍺🍺, **Great Easton,** *(just off the route)*
Plenty of choice in **Great Dunmow**
Cock and Bell Inn PH 🍺🍺, **High Easter**
The White Horse PH 🍺🍺, The Leather Bottle PH, **Pleshey**
The Swan Hotel PH, **Felsted**
Flitch of Bacon PH, **Little Dunmow,** *(just off the route)*
Red Lion PH, Kings Head PH, White Hart PH, **Stebbing**

Pleshey   Felsted   Stebbing   Lindsell

1 With back to the Guildhall in Thaxted, go down through the square on the B184 towards Great Dunmow, then 1st R at the end of the square on to Park Street (B1051) 'Broxted 3, Elsenham 6'

2 After 1½ km (1 mile), on sharp RH bend L by triangle of grass 'Duton Hill 2, The Eastons 3'

3 Follow signs for Dunmow for 7 km (4½ miles). At T-j with B184 R 'Dunmow 1'

4 At mini-roundabout SA 'Town Centre'. At T-j by Saracens Head Hotel L 'Chelmsford (A130)'

 two pages

16 At T-j with A120 R 'Chelmsford' then 1st L 'Stebbing 1'. Very busy section. **Take care**

17 After 1½ km (1 mile) 1st L in Stebbing by memorial cross 'Lindsell, Great Bardfield, Stebbing Village'

18 At T-j with B1507 R 'Lindsell 2¼, Great Bardfield 4¼'

19 After 2½ km (1½ miles), 1st L 'Lindsell'

20 At the end of buildings in Lindsell 1st R by triangle of grass 'Thaxted'

21 At T-j with B184 R 'Saffron Walden'.

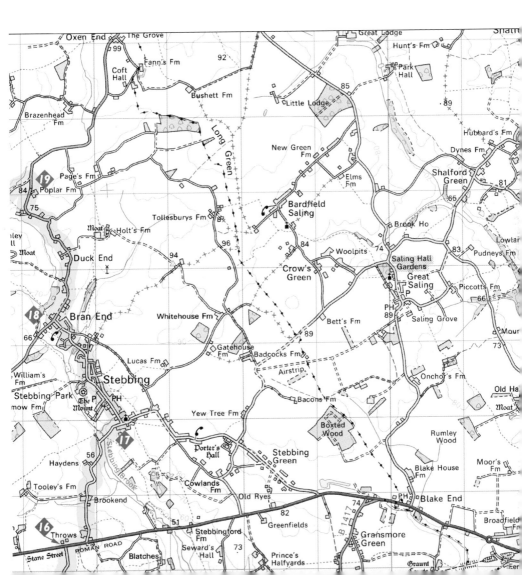

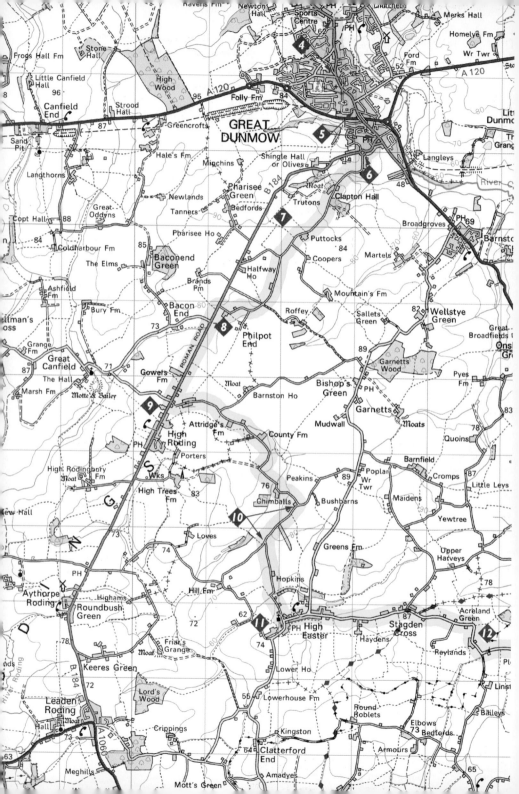

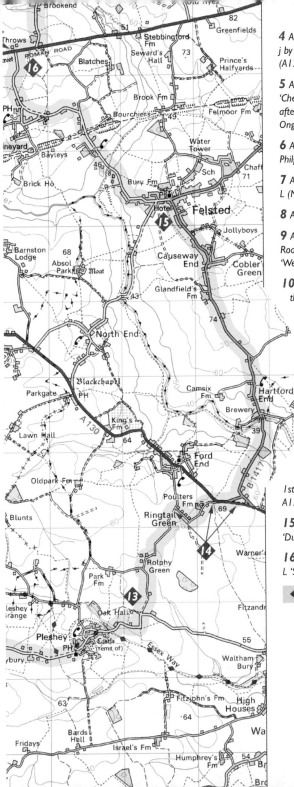

4 At mini-roundabout SA 'Town Centre'. At T-j by Saracens Head Hotel L 'Chelmsford (A130)'

5 At mini-roundabout at end of town SA 'Chelmsford, The Rodings, Ongar 14' then after 400 m (yd) R onto B184 'The Rodings, Ongar 14'

6 At roundabout L 'Clapton Hall, Puttocks, Philpot End'

7 At fork shortly after Mountain's Farm bear L (NS)

8 At T-j (with B184) L (NS)

9 After 1½ km (1 mile), at X-roads in High Roding by 30 MPH sign L onto Rands Road 'Wellstye Green, Barnston'

10 At T-j R 'High Easter, Leaden Roding' then 1st L by triangle of grass 'High Easter'

11 At T-j in High Easter L 'Pleshey, Dunmow'

12 **Easy to miss.** Follow signs for Pleshey for 3 km (2 miles). At triangle of grass L 'Pleshey, The Walthams'

13 800 m (½ mile) past Pleshey, on sharp RH bend by a triangle of grass L 'Ford End, Felsted'

14 **Easy to miss.** After 1½ km (1 mile) 1st R by red brick house (NS). At T-j with A130 R then 1st L on to B1417 'Felsted 2'

15 At T-j in Felsted by the Swan Hotel L 'Dunmow'

16 At T-j with A120 R 'Chelmsford' then 1st L 'Stebbing 1'. Very busy section. **Take care**

← two pages

8 Southwest from Sudbury to Castle Hedingham and the Belchamps

Start

The long-stay car park by the Leisure Pool in Sudbury, 24 km (15 miles) northwest of Colchester

P As above. Follow signs

Distance and grade

52 km (33 miles)
Easy / moderate

Terrain

Several climbs up to 30 m (100 ft). Lowest point – 22 m (75 ft) at Lamarsh. Highest point – 86 m (285 ft) near to Belchamp St Paul

Nearest railway

Sudbury

Although Sudbury lies in Suffolk, ninety per cent of this ride is in northern Essex. The ride starts by following the valley of the River Stour south through Henny Street, Lamarsh and the attractive village of Bures. Some of the farms on the tiny lanes southwest from Bures through Daw's Cross to Colne Engaine make you feel sure might have inspired Gainsborough, who was born in Sudbury. Halstead has few attractions for the cyclist and is avoided in favour of lanes that skirt to the north via the Maplesteads and Castle Hedingham. The route heads west as far as Toppesfield before returning towards Sudbury via the Belchamps.

Lavenham Bridge Street Shimpling Hartest Hawstead Sicklesmere

Sudbury 1

Birthplace of the painter Thomas Gainsborough in 1727. Half-timbered Gainsborough's House dates from 1480, with an added Georgian front. It is now a museum with portraits and landscapes illustrating the artist's career

Castle Hedingham 11

The village is dominated by the towering Norman keep of Hedingham Castle, built around 1140 by the De Vere family who lived here for 500 years. Well-preserved banqueting hall and minstrels' gallery

Colne Valley Railway 12

Vintage steam trains take passengers along a lovingly restored section of the Old Colne Valley and Halstead railway. There is a wildlife conservation area and picnic site

▲ *The Colne Valley Railway*

 Refreshments

Plenty of choice, Waggon and Horses PH 🍷, **Sudbury**
The Henny Swan PH 🍷🍷, **Henny Street**
The Red Lion PH 🍷🍷, **Lamarsh**
The Swan PH, The Eight Bells PH 🍷, **Bures**
The Bell PH 🍷🍷, **Castle Hedingham**
Waggon and Horses PH, The White Hart PH 🍷🍷,
Great Yeldham
Cherry Tree PH, **Knowl Green**
Half Moon PH 🍷🍷, **Belchamp St Paul**
Red Lion PH, **Belchamp Otter**

Gedding   Rattlesden   Hitcham

1 Turn L out of the car park. At T-j at the end of Station Road by the Anchor PH L. At T-j with A131 at the end of Church Street L 'Chelmsford, Halstead'

2 Cross bridge over river and go under railway bridge. At Kings Head PH 1st L on Middleton Road

➡ **three pages**

11 At T-j (with B1508) L 'Hedinghams', then after 800 m (½ mile), at start of Castle Hedingham 1st R onto Bayley Street 'Gt Yeldham, Haverhill, Hedingham Castle'

12 At X-roads with main road (A604) at end of Nunnery Street SA (NS)

13 At T-j by triangle of grass R 'Delvin End, Toppesfield'

14 At T-j R 'Toppesfield'

15 At T-j R 'Toppesfield'

16 At start of Toppesfield R onto Great Yeldham Road 'Gt Yeldham'.

17 At T-j with A604 L 'Cambridge' then 1st R after Post Office 'Little Yeldham 1, The Belchamps 4'

18 Follow signs for Belchamp St Paul for 5 km (3 miles). 800 m (½ mile) after the Half Moon PH in Belchamp St Paul 1st R onto Otter Road 'Belchamp Otter, Sudbury'

19 After 5 km (3 miles) at T-j L 'Borley, Sudbury'

20 At T-j L 'Sudbury'

21 At T-j (with A131) at the end of Bulmer Road L

22 Go under bridge then 1st R onto Church Street by the Old Bull Hotel

23 By the Anchor PH R on to Station Road to return to the start

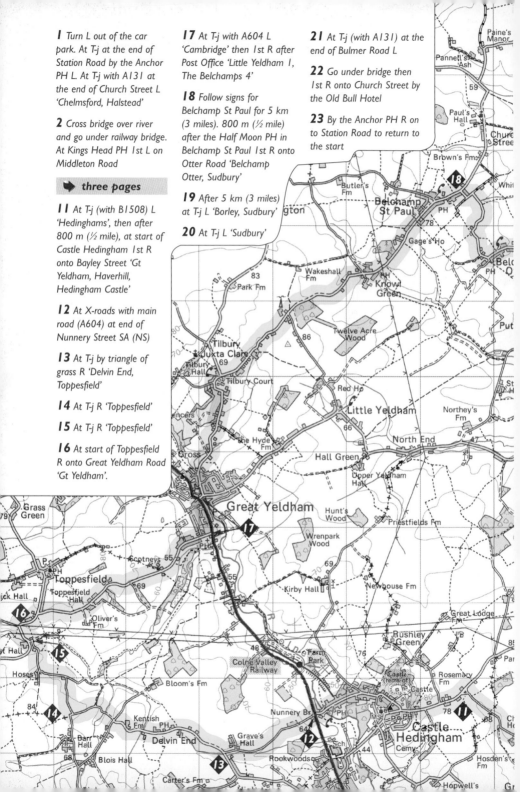

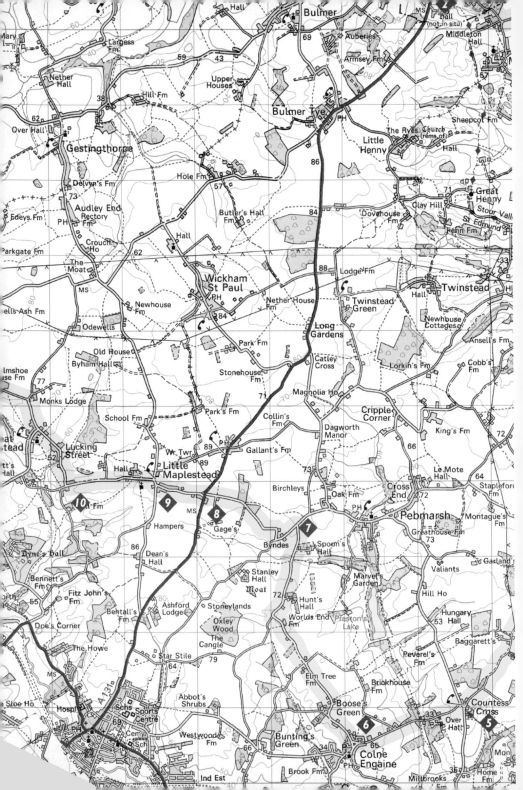

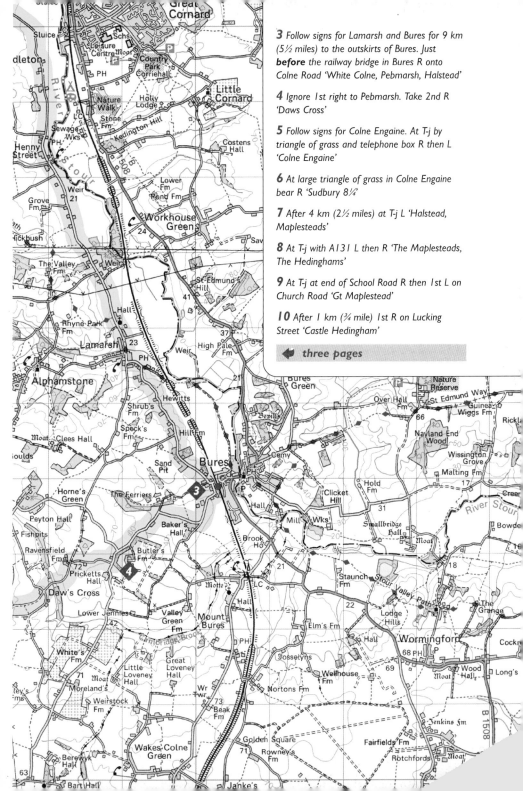

3 Follow signs for Lamarsh and Bures for 9 km (5½ miles) to the outskirts of Bures. Just **before** the railway bridge in Bures R onto Colne Road 'White Colne, Pebmarsh, Halstead'

4 Ignore 1st right to Pebmarsh. Take 2nd R 'Daws Cross'

5 Follow signs for Colne Engaine. At T-j by triangle of grass and telephone box R then L 'Colne Engaine'

6 At large triangle of grass in Colne Engaine bear R 'Sudbury 8¼'

7 After 4 km (2½ miles) at T-j L 'Halstead, Maplesteads'

8 At T-j with A131 L then R 'The Maplesteads, The Hedinghams'

9 At T-j at end of School Road R then 1st L on Church Road 'Gt Maplestead'

10 After 1 km (¾ mile) 1st R on Lucking Street 'Castle Hedingham'

← **three pages**

East from Saffron Walden through Thaxted, Finchingfield and the Bumpsteads

Three climbs south from Saffron Walden, one either side of the curiously named stream 'Fulfen Slade' and one from the crossroads north of Debden take you to

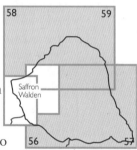

the attractive village of Thaxted with its very fine Guildhall. The ride heads west to two further pretty Essex villages – Great Bardfield and Finchingfield. The section on tiny lanes between the two villages is one of the highlights of the ride. The route turns north to Helions Bumpstead and Castle Camps before heading for home through Castle Camps and Ashdon.

Start

Cross Keys PH, near the traffic lights on the B184 Cambridge road, Saffron Walden, 29 km (18 miles) southeast of Cambridge

P Long-stay car park just off the B184 towards Cambridge

Distance and grade

51 km (32 miles)

Easy / moderate

Terrain

57 m (190 ft) climb from Audley End to Arkesden, 48 m (160 ft) climb southwest from Ashdon. Several shorter climbs. Lowest point – 50 m (165 ft) at Audley End. Highest point – 120 m (400 ft) at Castle Camps

Nearest railway

Audley End Station to the west of Saffron Walden is just off the route

Saffron Walden

Debden

Cutlers Green

Thaxted

Great Bardfield

▼ *Thaxted Guildhall*

Thaxted 3
Tudor houses surround the stately 14th-century Guildhall. The fine church dates from the 14th century. The elegant red-brick Clarence House, built in 1715, is where composer Gustav Holst worked on part of *The Planets*. The well-preserved tower windmill dating from 1804 has a museum of rural life

Great Bardfield 5
One of three Bardfield villages huddled by the River Pant, with medieval and Georgian houses, restored windmill, mainly 14th-century church, cottage museum and village lock-up

Finchingfield 8
Jumble of medieval cottages and Georgian houses around the village green

Refreshments

White Hart PH, Plough PH, **Debden**
Plenty of choice Swan PH 🍺, Star PH 🍺, **Thaxted**
The Bell PH, The Vine PH, **Great Bardfield**
Red Lion PH, Finchingfield Inn PH, Fox PH 🍺, **Finchingfield**
Three Horseshoes PH, **Helions Bumpstead**
Rose and Crown PH 🍺, **Ashdon**

Hempstead Wood

Helions Bumpstead

Castle Camps

Ashdon

1 With back to the Cross Keys PH L. At traffic lights SA. At mini-roundabout bear L onto Debden Road

2 After 5 km (3 miles) at offset X-roads SA 'Debden'.

3 After 8 km (5 miles), at T-j by church in Thaxted R 'Dunmow'

4 Through Thaxted. At far end of village L 'The Bardfields'.

5 At T-j with B1057 in Great Bardfield L 'Finchingfield 2, Steeple Bumpstead 7', then 1st R 'Braintree 9, Waltham's Cross' and 1st L after village stores 'Waltham's Cross 1'

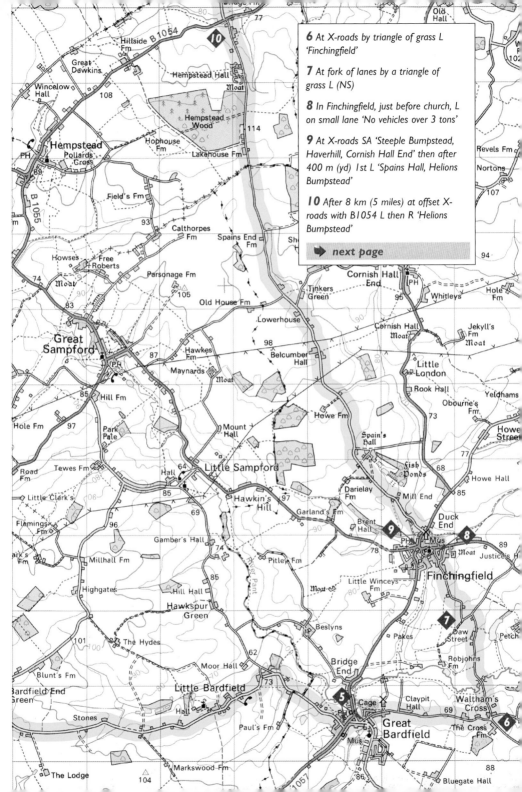

6 At X-roads by triangle of grass L 'Finchingfield'

7 At fork of lanes by a triangle of grass L (NS)

8 In Finchingfield, just before church, L on small lane 'No vehicles over 3 tons'

9 At X-roads SA 'Steeple Bumpstead, Haverhill, Cornish Hall End' then after 400 m (yd) 1st L 'Spains Hall, Helions Bumpstead'

10 After 8 km (5 miles) at offset X-roads with B1054 L then R 'Helions Bumpstead'

➡ *next page*

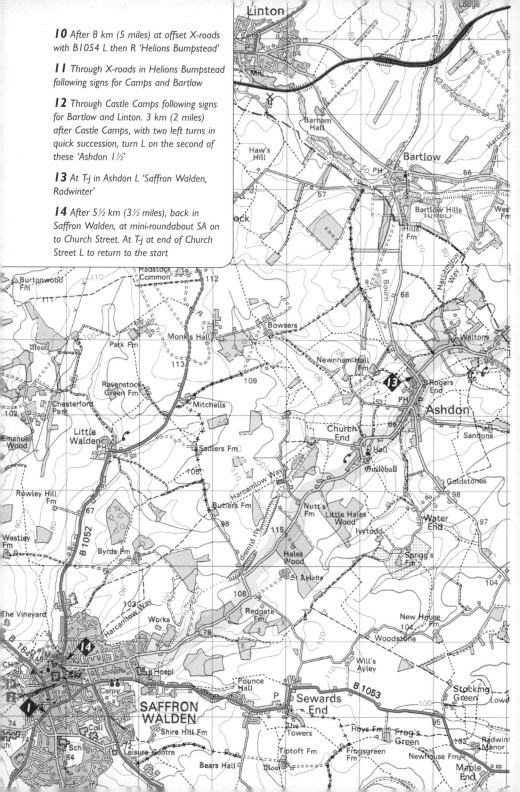

10 After 8 km (5 miles) at offset X-roads with B1054 L then R 'Helions Bumpstead'

11 Through X-roads in Helions Bumpstead following signs for Camps and Bartlow

12 Through Castle Camps following signs for Bartlow and Linton. 3 km (2 miles) after Castle Camps, with two left turns in quick succession, turn L on the second of these 'Ashdon 1½'

13 At T-j in Ashdon L 'Saffron Walden, Radwinter'

14 After 5½ km (3½ miles), back in Saffron Walden, at mini-roundabout SA on to Church Street. At T-j at end of Church Street L to return to the start

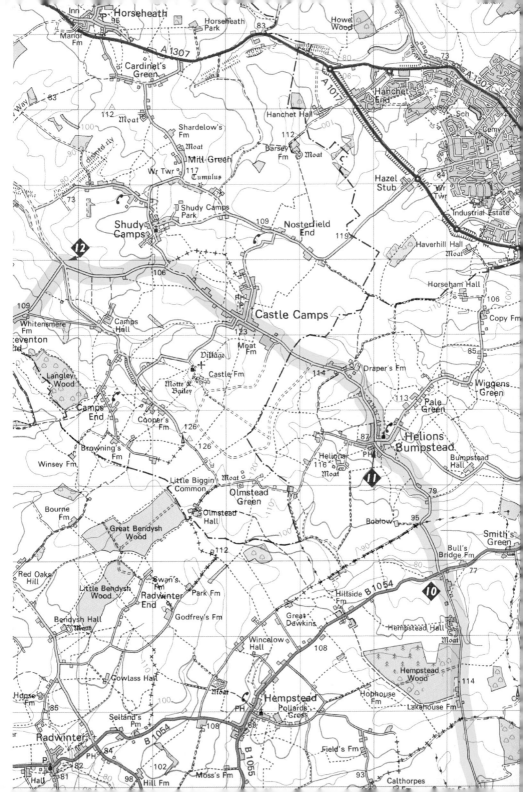

Southwest from Saffron Walden through pretty Essex villages of Arkesden, the Pelhams and Manuden

Start

Cross Keys PH, near the traffic lights on the B184 Cambridge road, Saffron Walden, 29 km (18 miles) south-east of Cambridge

P Long-stay car park just off the B184 towards Cambridge

Distance and grade

54 km (34 miles)
Easy / moderate

Terrain

57 m (190 ft) climb from Audley End towards Arkesden, several climbs of 30 m (100 ft). Lowest point – 50 m (165 ft) near Audley End. Highest point – 130 m (430 ft) near to Brent Pelham

Nearest railway

Audley End Station to the west of Saffron Walden is just off the route

Exiting Saffron Walden to the southwest, this ride soon reaches the lovely village of Arkesden, just the first in a string of attractive places along the way, most notably Clavering and

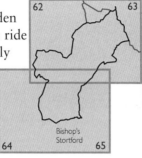

Manuden, all of them boasting a sprinkling of thatched cottages and flint walls. Some tiny quiet lanes are used to link up these villages, most memorably from Further Ford End through the Pelhams to Manuden and Rickling. If on a mountain bike, you may wish to try the sunken old lane that runs between Brent Pelham and Furneux Pelham. Otherwise, you must be content with a short spell on the truly delightful (vehicle-free) lane that loops back on itself around Hartham Common south of Brent Pelham. After all these idyllic lanes, the short section on the B183 comes as something of a shock but it is essentially downhill and you soon escape to the attractive village of Widdington before heading back to the start.

Saffron Walden

Arkesden

Clavering

Brent Pelham

Stocking Pelham

Clavering 6

A village of old cottages with moat encircling meadow where the Sherriff of Essex built a castle in 1052. One of Britain's smallest houses stands by the river

▲ *Thatchers at work in Arkesden*

Brent Pelham 9

The local hero is a certain Piers Shonks, famed for dragon-slaying, who was buried in the church walls. An inscription in the church reads:

'Shonks one serpent kills, t'other defies,

And in this wall as in a fortress lies'

Brent Pelham has medieval stocks and a whipping post

Furneux Pelham *(just off the route)* 11

The largest of the three Pelham villages once owned by the Norman family. The gloriously restored 15th-century church has windows by Morris and Burne-Jones. There is also a brewery and an adjacent pub, The Brewery Tap

Prior's Hall Barn, Widdington 19

Splendid aisled barn built from unseasoned oak beams, little altered since the 14th century

Mole Hall 19

Unusual mixture of animals from home and abroad, including wallabies, chimpanzees and otters. Wildfowl nest in the moat of the 13th-century manor house and there is a butterfly pavilion

> **Refreshments**

Plenty of choice, Eight Bells PH 🍴🍴, **Saffron Walden**
Axe and Compasses PH 🍴🍴, **Arkesden**
The Cricketers Inn PH 🍴, Fox and Hounds PH, **Clavering**
Black Horse PH, **Brent Pelham**
The Cock PH, **Stocking Pelham**
Brewery Tap PH 🍴, **Furneux Pelham,** *(just off the route)*
Catherine Wheel PH, **Gravesend**
Three Horseshoes PH, Yew Tree PH, **Manuden**
Cricketers Arms PH 🍴🍴, **Rickling Green**
Fleur de Lys PH 🍴, **Widdington**

Level's Green   Manuden   Quendon   Widdington   Debden Manor

1 With back to the Cross Keys PH L. At traffic lights SA up hill. At mini-roundabout SA. At next double mini-roundabout SA 'Audley End'

2 Just past the school on the left 1st L 'Wenden'

3 At T-j with B1383 L 'Newport, Bishop's Stortford' then 1st R on B1039 'Wendens Ambo, Royston 11'

4 At mini-roundabout SA over railway bridge then underneath motorway. 1 km (¾ mile) after going under M11, on sharp RH bend, next L 'Arkesden 1½'

5 At T-j by triangle of grass in Arkesden L 'Wicken Bonhunt, Clavering, Newport'

6 Follow signs for Clavering. At T-j with B1308 R 'Clavering ¾, Buntingford 9' then 2nd R in Clavering after the Fox and Hounds PH 'Ford'

7 Ignore two turnings to the right. 3 km (2 miles) out of Clavering 1st proper L 'Further Ford End. Unsuitable for motors'

8 At T-j by triangle of grass L 'Meesden, Brent Pelham'

9 At church and junction with B1038 bear L 'Newport' then 1st R 'Ford. Unsuitable for motors'

10 After 1 km (¾ mile) 1st L sharply back on yourself (**or** if you have a mountain bike you could go straight ahead and rejoin the route further south). At T-j R (NS)

11 At T-j in Stocking Pelham by The Cock PH R 'Furneux Pelham, Albury, Little Hadham'

➡ **two pages**

16 At T-j in Rickling Green L then 1st R 'Quendon ¼, Newport 3, Saffron Walden 6¼'

17 At T-j with B1383 L 'Newport, Saffron Walden'. Busy road

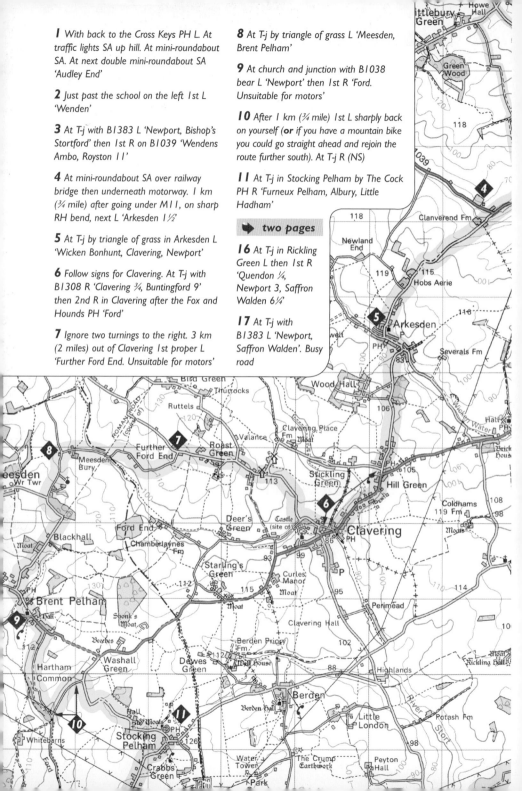

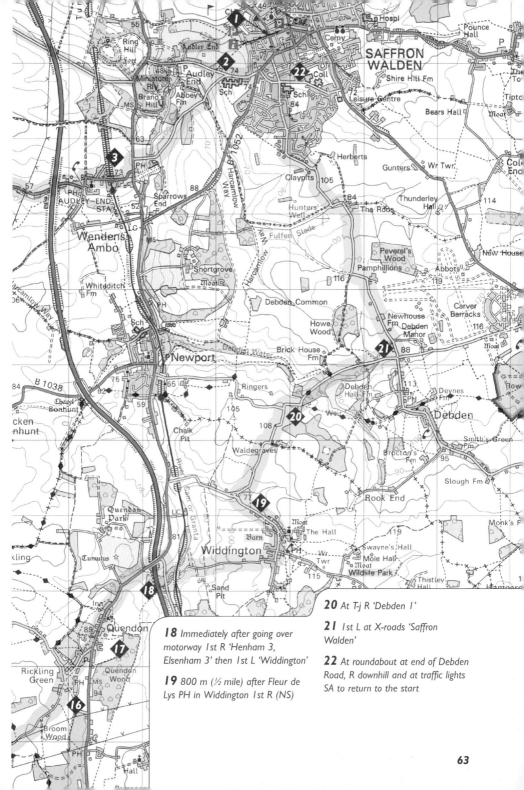

18 Immediately after going over motorway 1st R 'Henham 3, Elsenham 3' then 1st L 'Widdington'

19 800 m (½ mile) after Fleur de Lys PH in Widdington 1st R (NS)

20 At T-j R 'Debden 1'

21 1st L at X-roads 'Saffron Walden'

22 At roundabout at end of Debden Road, R downhill and at traffic lights SA to return to the start

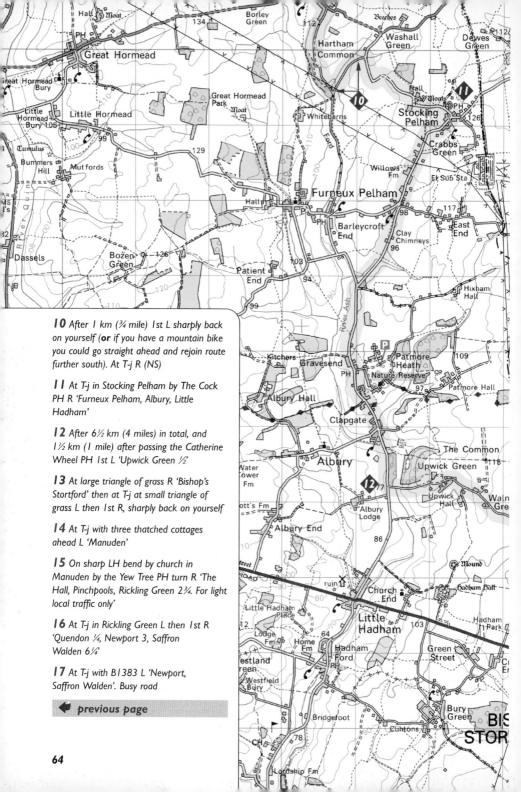

10 After 1 km (¾ mile) 1st L sharply back on yourself (**or** if you have a mountain bike you could go straight ahead and rejoin route further south). At T-j R (NS)

11 At T-j in Stocking Pelham by The Cock PH R 'Furneux Pelham, Albury, Little Hadham'

12 After 6½ km (4 miles) in total, and 1½ km (1 mile) after passing the Catherine Wheel PH 1st L 'Upwick Green ½'

13 At large triangle of grass R 'Bishop's Stortford' then at T-j at small triangle of grass L then 1st R, sharply back on yourself

14 At T-j with three thatched cottages ahead L 'Manuden'

15 On sharp LH bend by church in Manuden by the Yew Tree PH turn R 'The Hall, Pinchpools, Rickling Green 2¾. For light local traffic only'

16 At T-j in Rickling Green L then 1st R 'Quendon ¼, Newport 3, Saffron Walden 6¼'

17 At T-j with B1383 L 'Newport, Saffron Walden'. Busy road

◀ previous page

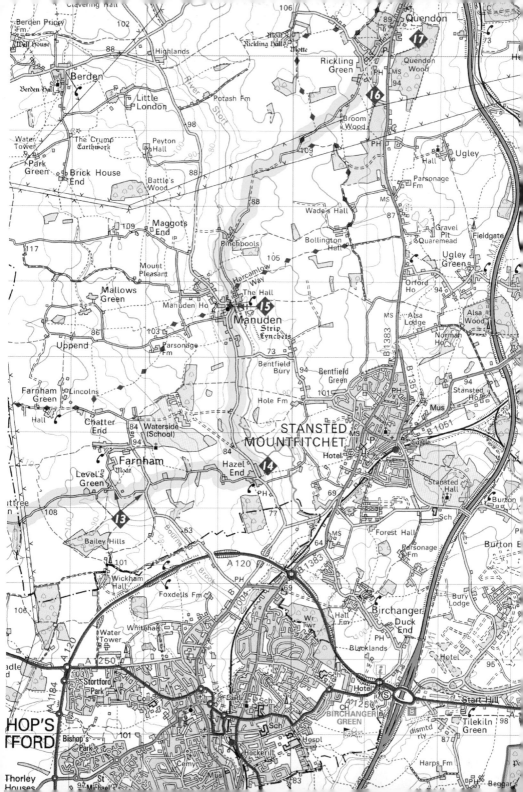

Northwest from Saffron Walden along the valley of the Cam to Barrington

 Start

Cross Keys PH, near
the traffic lights on the
B184 Cambridge road,
Saffron Walden, 29 km
(18 miles) southeast of
Cambridge

P Long-stay car park
just off the B184
towards Cambridge

 Distance and grade

52 km (33 miles)
Easy / moderate

Terrain

73 m (240 ft) climb
west from Littlebury.
51 m (170 ft) climb
south from Haslingfield.
76 m (250 ft) climb
southeast from
Fowlmere. Lowest
point – 13 m (45 ft)
near to Haslingfield.
Highest point – 110 m
(370 ft) to the west of
Littlebury

 Nearest railway

Audley End Station to
the west of Saffron
Walden is just off the
route

The course of the Icknield Way east from Royston represents the edge of the chalk and flint escarpment that runs from Dunstable to Newmarket and on to the coast. To the north and west of this lies the start of the lowlands that become the Fens further north. The River Cam or Rhee is crossed near Haslingfield at 13 m (45 ft) above sea level, so the land to the north falls only 13 m (45 ft) in the next 80 km (50 miles) as the Cam joins the River Great Ouse and empties its waters into The Wash north of King's Lynn. The ride follows the string of villages along the River Cam or Granta to the north of Saffron Walden, then crosses into the valley of the other main tributary of the Cam, passing several fine pubs along the way. The cement works at Barrington strike an incongruous note in a ride along otherwise quiet lanes, through fine arable country. A steady climb south from Fowlmere takes you to over 91 m (300 ft) before dropping down to the beautiful stately home at Audley End just to the west of the start.

70   71

68   69

Saffron Walden

Saffron Walden   Littlebury   Hinxton   Whittlesford   Newton

▼ Pargeting on the old Sun Inn, Saffron Walden

Saffron Walden 1
The town is dominated by the 59 metre (193 ft) spire of Essex's largest church. The Saffron crocus, grown for the

yellow dye used to colour cloth and cakes, brought prosperity for 400 years. There are myriad 15th- and 16th-century buildings decorated with elaborate plasterwork known as 'pargeting'

Ickleton 5
The Normans made use of Roman tiles and columns when building the unusual parish church. There are strange beasts carved upon the pews and the churchyard wall

Duxford 10
The Imperial War Museum houses a superb collection of historic aircraft ranging from First World War fighters to the first Concorde ever flown

Docwra's Manor, Shepreth 15
Exotic plants spill out of raised beds, stone troughs and old sinks in 2 acres of inventive garden design

Fowlmere Nature Reserve 16
Oasis for resident warblers and kingfishers in an 85 acre fen reed bed with boardwalks and hides

Refreshments

Plenty of choice, Eight Bells PH 🍷🍷, **Saffron Walden**
Ickleton Lion PH, **Ickleton**
Red Lion PH 🍷🍷, **Hinxton**
Wheatsheaf PH, John Barleycorn PH 🍷🍷, **Duxford**
Bees in the Wall PH, **Whittlesford**
Queens Head PH 🍷🍷, **Newton**
Royal Oak PH 🍷🍷, **Barrington**
Chequers Inn PH 🍷🍷, Swan Inn PH, Queens Head PH 🍷🍷, **Fowlmere**

Audley End 22
Mainly Georgian village with Jacobean almshouses. Audley End House was built in 1603 for the 1st Earl of Suffolk and has much fine decorative work by Adam. The classical grounds were landscaped by Capability Brown

Barrington

Fowlmere

Strethall

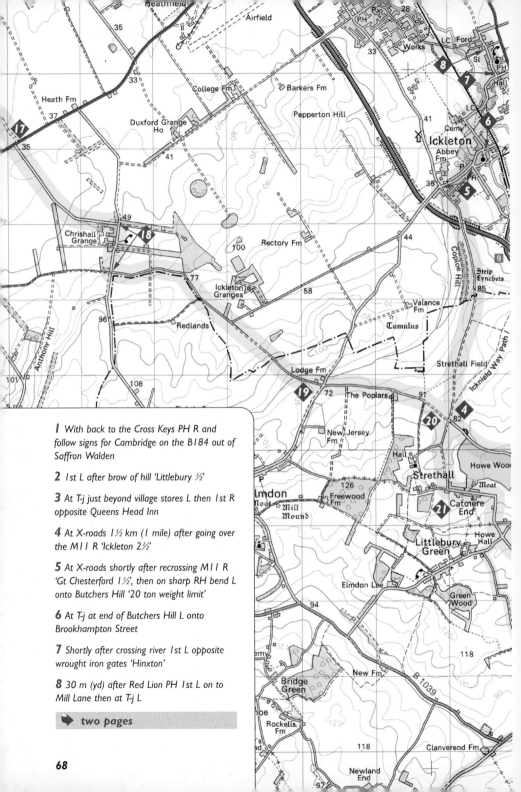

1 With back to the Cross Keys PH R and follow signs for Cambridge on the B184 out of Saffron Walden

2 1st L after brow of hill 'Littlebury ½'

3 At T-j just beyond village stores L then 1st R opposite Queens Head Inn

4 At X-roads 1½ km (1 mile) after going over the M11 R 'Ickleton 2½'

5 At X-roads shortly after recrossing M11 R 'Gt Chesterford 1½', then on sharp RH bend L onto Butchers Hill '20 ton weight limit'

6 At T-j at end of Butchers Hill L onto Brookhampton Street

7 Shortly after crossing river 1st L opposite wrought iron gates 'Hinxton'

8 30 m (yd) after Red Lion PH 1st L on to Mill Lane then at T-j L

➡ **two pages**

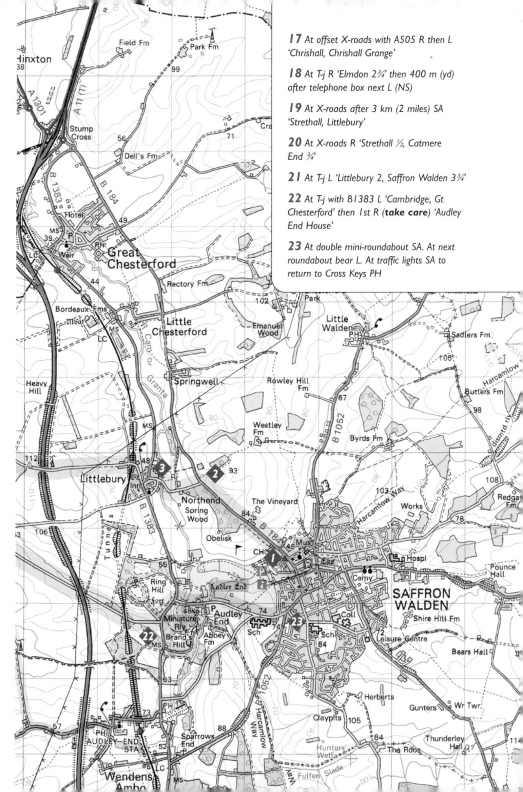

17 At offset X-roads with A505 R then L 'Chrishall, Chrishall Grange'

18 At T-j R 'Elmdon 2¾' then 400 m (yd) after telephone box next L (NS)

19 At X-roads after 3 km (2 miles) SA 'Strethall, Littlebury'

20 At X-roads R 'Strethall ½, Catmere End ¾'

21 At T-j L 'Littlebury 2, Saffron Walden 3¾'

22 At T-j with B1383 L 'Cambridge, Gt Chesterford' then 1st R (**take care**) 'Audley End House'

23 At double mini-roundabout SA. At next roundabout bear L. At traffic lights SA to return to Cross Keys PH

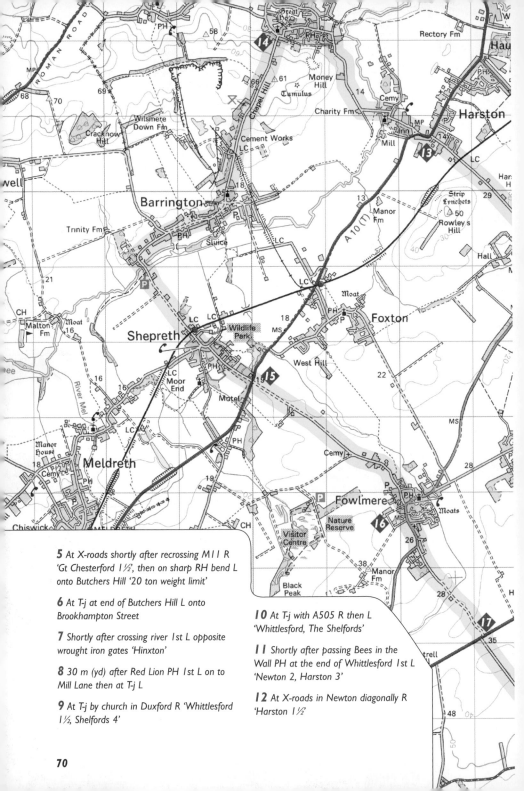

5 At X-roads shortly after recrossing M11 R 'Gt Chesterford 1½', then on sharp RH bend L onto Butchers Hill '20 ton weight limit'

6 At T-j at end of Butchers Hill L onto Brookhampton Street

7 Shortly after crossing river 1st L opposite wrought iron gates 'Hinxton'

8 30 m (yd) after Red Lion PH 1st L on to Mill Lane then at T-j L

9 At T-j by church in Duxford R 'Whittlesford 1½, Shelfords 4'

10 At T-j with A505 R then L 'Whittlesford, The Shelfords'

11 Shortly after passing Bees in the Wall PH at the end of Whittlesford 1st L 'Newton 2, Harston 3'

12 At X-roads in Newton diagonally R 'Harston 1½'

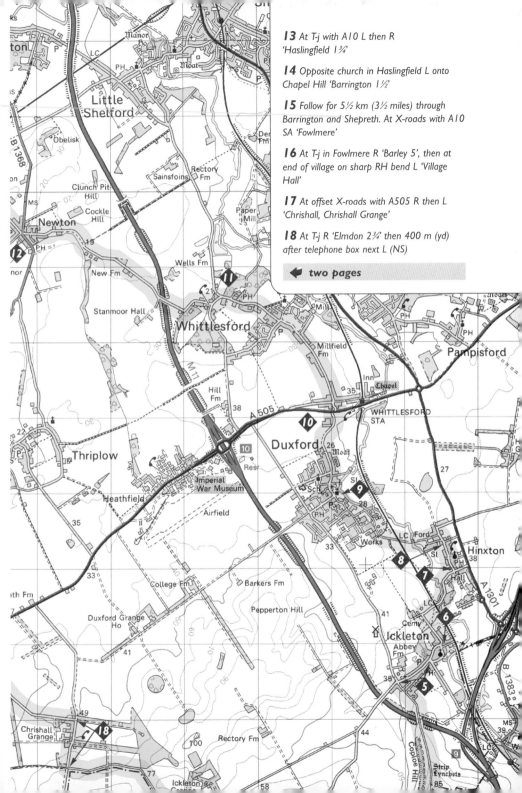

13 At T-j with A10 L then R 'Haslingfield 1¾'

14 Opposite church in Haslingfield L onto Chapel Hill 'Barrington 1½'

15 Follow for 5½ km (3½ miles) through Barrington and Shepreth. At X-roads with A10 SA 'Fowlmere'

16 At T-j in Fowlmere R 'Barley 5', then at end of village on sharp RH bend L 'Village Hall'

17 At offset X-roads with A505 R then L 'Chrishall, Chrishall Grange'

18 At T-j R 'Elmdon 2¾' then 400 m (yd) after telephone box next L (NS)

◄ **two pages**

12 East from St Neots through open farmland to Great Gransden and Conington

Gentle riding along quiet lanes through undulating arable country characterises this ride to the east of St Neots.

Start

The Old Falcon Hotel, the Market Square, St Neots

P Several long-stay car parks, follow signs

Distance and grade

52 km (33 miles)

Easy

Terrain

No major hills. Lowest point – 10 m (35 ft) at Hilton. Highest point – 70 m (230 ft) northeast of Bourn

Nearest railway

St Neots

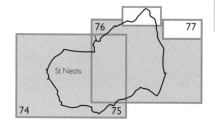

Refreshments

Plenty of choice, River Mill PH 🍴, **St Neots**
Duncombe Arms PH, **Waresley**
Crown and Cushion PH 🍴, **Great Gransden**
Duke of Wellington PH 🍴, **Bourn**
White Swan PH 🍴, **Conington**
Three Horseshoes PH, **Graveley**

St Neots   Crane Hill   Lily Hill   Waresley   Great Gransden   Caxton   Bourn

Bourn Windmill 7
Pre-Civil War post mill, which may well be the oldest of its type in England and was thoroughly restored in the 1980s

Conington 10
The church of St Mary has a 14th-century tower, 18th-century nave and late 19th-century chancel. Monuments to the Cotton family include one by famous woodcarver Grinling Gibbons

Fenstanton *(just off the route)* 11
The landscape genius Capability Brown (1715–83) is buried in the 14th-century village church that stands among colour-washed cottages and Georgian houses

Hemingford Grey *(just off the route)* 11
A village of timber, thatch and brick cottages. The moated Norman manor house is said to be the oldest inhabited home in England. The upper section of the 12th-century church spire came down in a gale in 1741 and is believed to be at the bottom of the river

Knapwell

Fenstanton

Hilton

Graveley

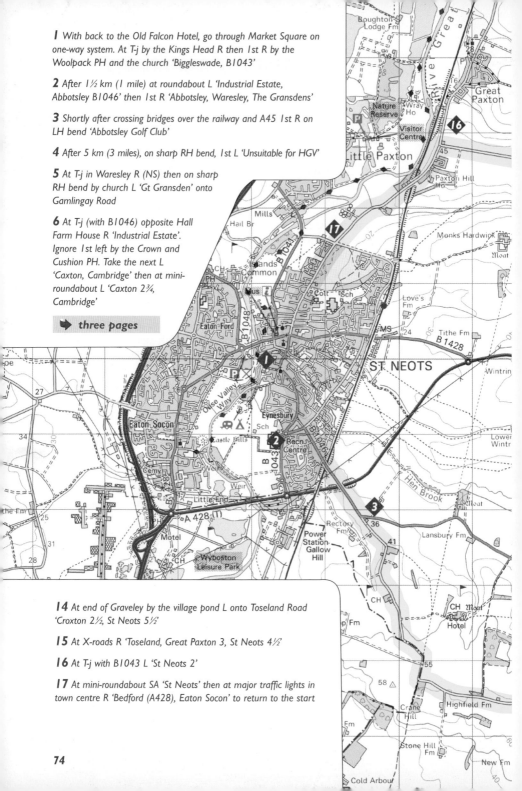

1 With back to the Old Falcon Hotel, go through Market Square on one-way system. At T-j by the Kings Head R then 1st R by the Woolpack PH and the church 'Biggleswade, B1043'

2 After 1½ km (1 mile) at roundabout L 'Industrial Estate, Abbotsley B1046' then 1st R 'Abbotsley, Waresley, The Gransdens'

3 Shortly after crossing bridges over the railway and A45 1st R on LH bend 'Abbotsley Golf Club'

4 After 5 km (3 miles), on sharp RH bend, 1st L 'Unsuitable for HGV'

5 At T-j in Waresley R (NS) then on sharp RH bend by church L 'Gt Gransden' onto Gamlingay Road

6 At T-j (with B1046) opposite Hall Farm House R 'Industrial Estate'. Ignore 1st left by the Crown and Cushion PH. Take the next L 'Caxton, Cambridge' then at mini-roundabout L 'Caxton 2¾, Cambridge'

➡ **three pages**

14 At end of Graveley by the village pond L onto Toseland Road 'Croxton 2½, St Neots 5½'

15 At X-roads R 'Toseland, Great Paxton 3, St Neots 4½'

16 At T-j with B1043 L 'St Neots 2'

17 At mini-roundabout SA 'St Neots' then at major traffic lights in town centre R 'Bedford (A428), Eaton Socon' to return to the start

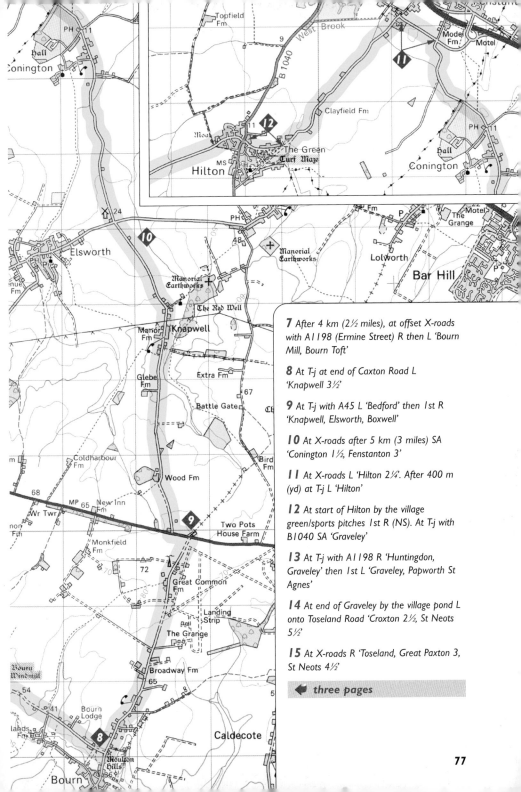

7 After 4 km (2½ miles), at offset X-roads with A1198 (Ermine Street) R then L 'Bourn Mill, Bourn Toft'

8 At T-j at end of Caxton Road L 'Knapwell 3½'

9 At T-j with A45 L 'Bedford' then 1st R 'Knapwell, Elsworth, Boxwell'

10 At X-roads after 5 km (3 miles) SA 'Conington 1½, Fenstanton 3'

11 At X-roads L 'Hilton 2¼'. After 400 m (yd) at T-j L 'Hilton'

12 At start of Hilton by the village green/sports pitches 1st R (NS). At T-j with B1040 SA 'Graveley'

13 At T-j with A1198 R 'Huntingdon, Graveley' then 1st L 'Graveley, Papworth St Agnes'

14 At end of Graveley by the village pond L onto Toseland Road 'Croxton 2½, St Neots 5½'

15 At X-roads R 'Toseland, Great Paxton 3, St Neots 4½'

◀ **three pages**

13 From St Neots to Grafham Water and south to Thurleigh

This ride visits Grafham Water: one of the most popular cycling attractions in the region. As with Rutland Water, some 48 km (30 miles) to the northwest, a route has been designed around the reservoir, using improved existing rights of way and quiet lanes to form a most satisfying circular ride of appeal to everyone – from children just learning to ride to adults who may be returning to cycling after many years' absence. This ride follows the loop around the reservoir for about two-thirds of its length before turning southwest along quiet lanes to Keysoe and Thurleigh. The route turns east here crossing gently undulating arable land to return via Duloe beneath the A1 back to St Neots.

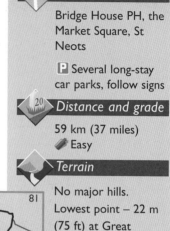

Start

Bridge House PH, the Market Square, St Neots

P Several long-stay car parks, follow signs

Distance and grade

59 km (37 miles)

Easy

Terrain

No major hills. Lowest point – 22 m (75 ft) at Great Staughton. Highest point – 82 m (270 ft) at Thurleigh

Nearest railway

St Neots

Refreshments

Plenty of choice, River Mill PH ●, **St Neots**
The Horseshoe PH, The Swan PH, **Offord Cluny**
Old Lion and Lamb PH, The Vine PH,
The George PH, **Buckden**
Plenty of choice around **Grafham Water**
Chequers PH ●●, **Keysoe**
The Olde Plough PH ●●, **Bolnhurst**
The Wheatsheaf PH, **Roothams Green**

St Neots   Great Paxton   Buckden   Grafham   West Perry   Great Staughton

St Neots 1
St Neots grew up around a 12th-century Benedictine Priory. In the 17th and 18th centuries, there was much rebuilding in the town – the river was dredged, and sluices were built enabling goods to be brought in by water. The magnificent church tower soars above the market square framed by Georgian houses backing onto the Great Ouse

Buckden Towers 4
Former moated ecclesiastical palace of the Bishops of Lincoln with a splendid 15th-century gatehouse and tower. Queen Catherine of Aragon was imprisoned here before being taken to Kimbolton Castle

Grafham Water 5
The circuit of the lake is one of the best family cycle routes in the region. It is also a woodland nature reserve providing nesting sites for lapwings, skylarks, wagtails, willow warblers and chiff chaffs

Kimbolton (just off the route) 9
A village with a Tudor manor remodelled in 1707 by Sir John Vanbrugh. Catherine of Aragon was imprisoned here after being divorced by Henry VIII. The church has some fine monuments

Bushmead Priory (just off the route) 16
A small Augustinian priory founded in 1195. Magnificent 13th-century timber roof of crown post construction with medieval wall paintings and stained glass

Brook End

Thurleigh

Rootham's Green

Duloe

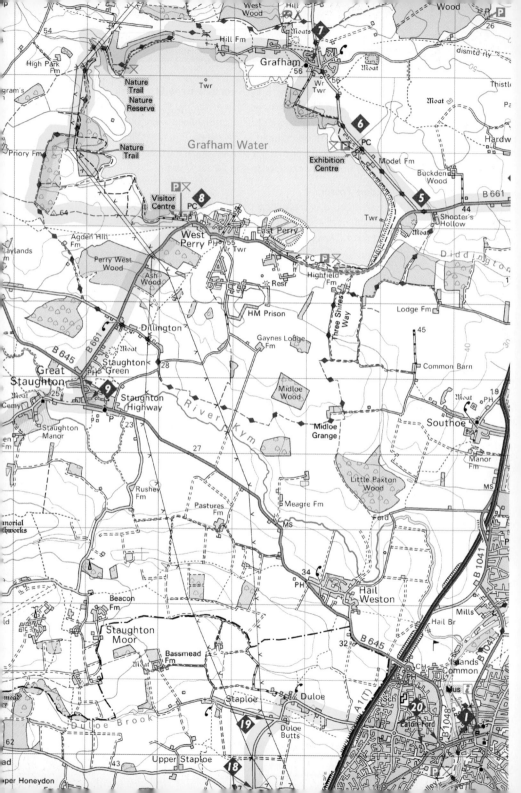

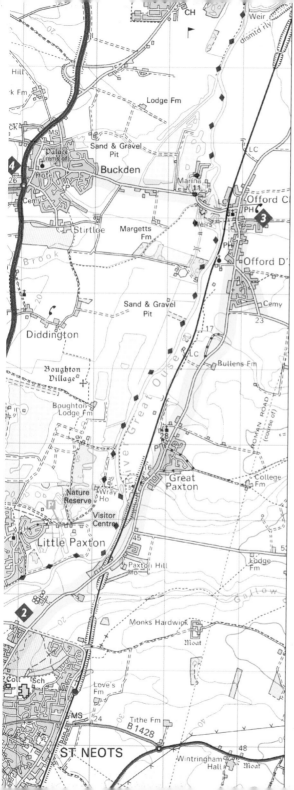

1 With back to Bridge House PH, Market Square, turn L away from the bridge. At 2nd major traffic lights (i.e. ignore pelican crossings) L onto Huntingdon Street 'Great Paxton. Priory Centre'

2 At roundabout SA following signs for Great Paxton then Offord Cluny.

3 Go past The Horseshoe PH in Offord Cluny. Just by the Swan PH L 'Buckden 1½'

4 At T-j in Buckden at the end of Church Street L (NS) then at roundabout with A1 SA 'Kimbolton B661'. **Take care** on the roundabout. Signal clearly and ride confidently

5 After 1½ km (1 mile) 1st R 'Grafham 1½, Ellington 3'

6 At car park sign after 1½ km (1 mile) L into Marlow car park. Go SA towards lake and turn R on to the obvious cycle track

7 At T-j at the end of the track (Church Hill) in Grafham L and follow the tarmac to the end. Continue on the cycle track around the lake

8 At the car park (Mander Park), follow cycle signs to the main road. At the T-j with the B661 R (i.e. leave the round-the-lake ride at this point)

9 At T-j with the A45 L 'St Neots, Hail Weston' then on sharp LH bend 1st R 'Little Staughton, Pertenhall'

➡ **next page**

18 At T-j R 'Eaton Socon 1, St Neots 3'. At next T-j R (same sign) then after 300 m (yd) 1st L 'Duloe 1'

19 At T-j R 'Eaton Socon 1½, St Neots 2'

20 At X-roads SA onto Mill Hill Road. At mini-roundabout by Royce Court L then at major roundabout SA 'Town Centre B1428'

9 At T-j with the A45 L 'St Neots, Hail Weston' then on sharp LH bend 1st R 'Little Staughton, Pertenhall'

10 After 5 km (3 miles) at T-j with B660 L 'Keysoe 1½, Bedford 11'

11 Ignore 1st right by Chequers Inn. Take next R near to the top of short hill onto Church Road 'Keysoe, Hatch End 1'

12 Ignore 1st right to Keysoe End West. Take next R by pair of thatched cottages onto Hatch Lane 'Thurleigh 2¾'

13 At T-j in Thurleigh L 'Bolnhurst 2¼, Keysoe 4¾'

14 At T-j with B660 R 'Bedford 6½, Bolnhurst Top End, Ravensden 3½'

15 After 1½ km (1 mile) 1st L on New Road 'Colmworth 1¾, Little Staughton 5'

16 At T-j at end of New Road L 'Colmworth 1, Bushmead 1¾, Little Staughton 3½' then after 300 m (yd) 1st R on Mill Road 'Colesden 2½, Wyboston 4'

17 Easy to miss. After 6½ km (4 miles), on sharp RH bend, take the 2nd L 'Staploe 2½, Duloe 2½'

18 At T-j R 'Eaton Socon 1, St Neots 3'. At next T-j R (same sign) then after 300 m (yd) 1st L 'Duloe 1'

19 At T-j R 'Eaton Socon 1½, St Neots 2'

◀ previous page

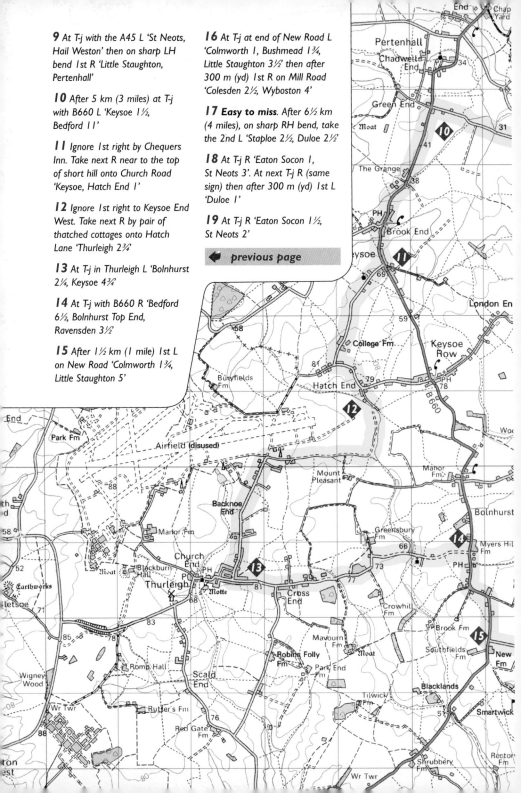

East from Ewelme into the Chiltern beechwoods

Ewelme's collection of 15th-century buildings make it one of the prettiest villages in the Chilterns. One has the impression of leaving the plains and heading for the hills as the route crosses open arable farmland to join the Ridgeway, claimed to be one of the oldest roads in Europe, dating back some 5000 years. At this point, it is also known as the Icknield Way, named after the Iceni tribe that inhabited Norfolk before the arrival of the Romans. The track climbs steeply through Howe Wood up to Cookley Green – the highest point on the ride. After Russell's Water, you enter the secret kingdom of the Chilterns with a lofty canopy of beech trees covering the steep hillsides and dry valleys linked by a magnificent network of bridleways. After the steady climb to Park Corner, the trail becomes slightly less defined on its gentle descent through woodland back into the open farmland that characterises the start of the ride.

Start

The car park by the playing fields in Ewelme, a village 5 km (3 miles) northeast of Wallingford

P As above – the car park is on the southeast edge of Ewelme on the minor road from Ewelme towards Swyncombe and Cookley Green

Distance and grade

24 km (15 miles)

 Strenuous

Terrain

Farmland and beechwoods. Three climbs - a 131 m (430 ft) climb from Ewelme to Cookley Green; 70 m (230 ft) between Pishill and Maidensgrove; 91 m (300 ft) between Maidensgrove and Park Corner. Lowest point – 91 m (300 ft) in Ewelme. Highest point – 222 m (730 ft) at Cookley Green

Ewelme

Dame Alice Farm

Russell's Water

Nearest railway

Henley-on-Thames, 10 km (6 miles) south-east of the route near Maidensgrove (12)

Places of interest

Ewelme 1
One of the most picturesque of the Chiltern villages with a group of 15th-century buildings. The church is notable for the tomb of Chaucer's granddaughter, Alice, Duchess of Suffolk. Her double effigy is an excellent example of medieval craftsmanship. The school has been in use since 1437. The grave of Jerome K. Jerome lies in the churchyard

Refreshments

Ploughman PH 🍺,
Shepherds Hut PH 🍺,
Ewelme
*Crown PH 🍺🍺, **Pishill***
Pubs off the route at
***Stonor, Bix** 🍺🍺 and*
***Nettlebed** 🍺*

As with all rides in the Chilterns, this can be very tough going from late autumm to late spring when many of the tracks turn to mud

Maidensgrove

Park Corner

Potters Farm

1 Exit car park and bear diagonally L on the upper road 'Britwell Salome 2, Watlington 3½'. At T-j on sharp bend bear R 'Britwell 2, Watlington 3½'

2 **Easy to miss.** 400 m (yd) after the end of the village, shortly after start of climb, turn R onto track 'Right of Way'

3 The rough track improves. Go past farm. Ignore the 1st track to the left. At X-roads of tracks (with the road 50 m (yd) to the right) turn L 'Right of Way'

4 At X-roads with road SA

5 At 5-way junction shortly after two red-brick houses turn sharp R on tarmac lane 'Bridleway' (blue arrow). Follow past farm and onto woodland track climbing steadily

6 At T-j with broad gravel track L then at T-j with road L again

7 At T-j with B480 R. Ignore 1st left to Stonor. Take next L 'Russell's Water ¾, Maidensgrove 2'

8 Shortly after a row of red-brick houses and telephone box in Russell's Water turn L by triangle of grass and village pond onto track. Follow broad gravel track as it swings L past farm and between barns. Go SA onto narrow grassy track which soon improves, following white arrows

9 At T-j of tracks near to house turn R 'PS17' (blue arrow) (**Or** for the pub in Pishill turn L here. Return to this point)

10 Fine views. Steep descent then climb. Continue on track through woodland following white arrows and ignoring turnings to the left then right. At T-j with road R

11 Ignore left turn on no through road to Maidensgrove. Exit woodland onto wide, flat, grassy area. On sharp RH bend leave road and turn L onto track 'Right of Way'

12 Excellent descent. At X-roads of tracks at the bottom R

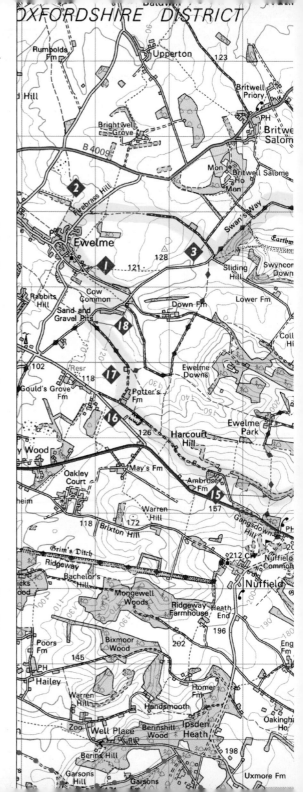

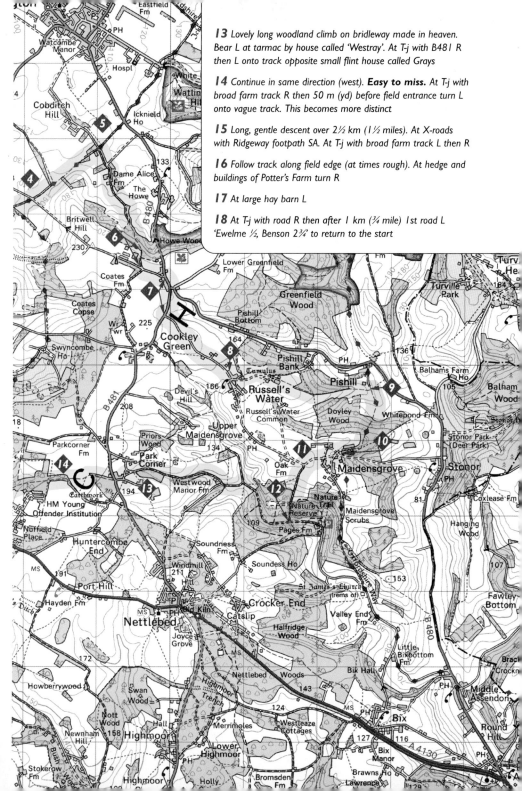

13 Lovely long woodland climb on bridleway made in heaven. Bear L at tarmac by house called 'Westray'. At T-j with B481 R then L onto track opposite small flint house called Grays

14 Continue in same direction (west). **Easy to miss.** At T-j with broad farm track R then 50 m (yd) before field entrance turn L onto vague track. This becomes more distinct

15 Long, gentle descent over 2½ km (1½ miles). At X-roads with Ridgeway footpath SA. At T-j with broad farm track L then R

16 Follow track along field edge (at times rough). At hedge and buildings of Potter's Farm turn R

17 At large hay barn L

18 At T-j with road R then after 1 km (¾ mile) 1st road L 'Ewelme ½, Benson 2¾' to return to the start

From Hambleden into the heart of the Chilterns

As with so much of the off-road cycling in the Chilterns, it is astonishing how far you feel from the built-up southeast of England on this ride. Only 48 km (30 miles) from central London, you could easily convince yourself you are deep in the West Country. The ride starts from near the Thames at Mill End and climbs on-road for 5½ km (3½ miles) through Rotten Row and Rockwell End to Parmoor. A superb descent follows, dropping down through Hatchet Wood to Skirmett and Fingest, with both villages boasting of fine pubs. Three steep climbs and descents in and out of the beechwoods take you to Northend and the highest point on the ride. Appropriately, this is followed by the longest descent, down to Stonor and then the steepest climb alongside the park boundary. From the top, the views across the Thames Valley to the southeast are magnificent and with the exception of a very short climb near to the end the rest of the ride is all downhill.

Start

The car park 5 km (3 miles) northeast of Henley-on-Thames (off A4155 Marlow road) on the minor road towards Hambleden and Skirmett

P As above

Distance and grade

29 km (18 miles)

///// Strenuous

Terrain

Steep beech-clad Chiltern hills. Five climbs – 131 m (430 ft) from Hambleden to Parmoor; 109 m (360 ft) from Fingest to Hanger Wood; 100 m (330 ft) through Harecramp Estate to Ibstone; 91 m (300 ft) up to Northend; 100 m (330 ft) up from Stonor. Lowest point - 39 m (130 ft) at the start. Highest point - 222 m (730 ft) west of Northend

Nearest railway

Henley-on-Thames, 5 km (3 miles) from the start

Mill End   Rotten Row   Rockwell End   Skirmett   Hanger Wood   Ibstone

Hambleden 1
Brick and flint village noted for its grand 14th-century church and its picturesque square with a water pump beneath a spreading chestnut tree. Until 1956, the pump was the village's main water supply. In the churchyard is a memorial to William Henry Smith, who built his family firm W H Smith into Britain's leading newsagent. A less successful son of Hambleden was the Earl of Cardigan who led the disastrous Charge of the Light Brigade in 1854

Fingest 6
An attractive village of brick and timber houses, dominated by the tower of St Bartholomew's Church whose unique, double-saddleback roof gives the whole village a slightly foreign air. The tower is early Norman with tiny windows like those of a fortress with its thick walls

▼ Hambleden

Refreshments

Stag & Huntsman PH 🍴🍺, **Hambleden**
Old Crown PH 🍴🍺, Frog PH, **Skirmett**
Chequers PH 🍴🍺, **Fingest**
Bull & Butcher 🍴🍺, **Turville**
Fox PH 🍺, **Ibstone**
White Hart PH 🍴🍺, **Northend**

Northend

Stonor

Great Wood

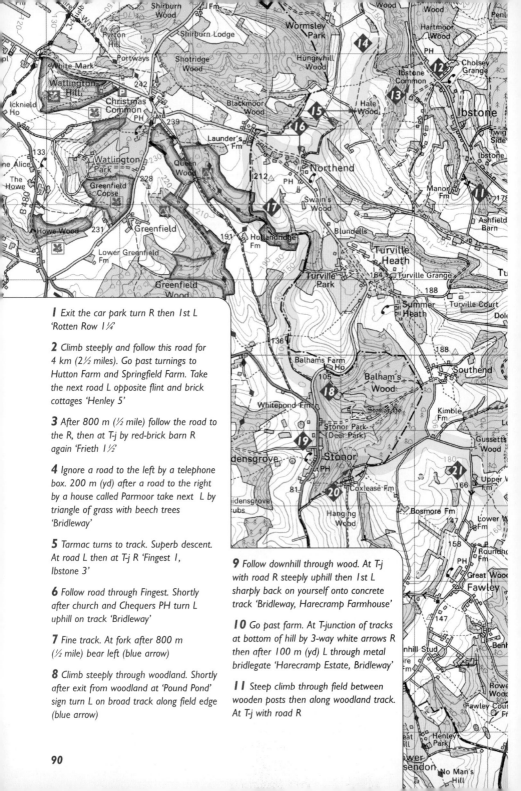

1 Exit the car park turn R then 1st L 'Rotten Row 1¼'

2 Climb steeply and follow this road for 4 km (2½ miles). Go past turnings to Hutton Farm and Springfield Farm. Take the next road L opposite flint and brick cottages 'Henley 5'

3 After 800 m (½ mile) follow the road to the R, then at T-j by red-brick barn R again 'Frieth 1½'

4 Ignore a road to the left by a telephone box. 200 m (yd) after a road to the right by a house called Parmoor take next L by triangle of grass with beech trees 'Bridleway'

5 Tarmac turns to track. Superb descent. At road L then at T-j R 'Fingest 1, Ibstone 3'

6 Follow road through Fingest. Shortly after church and Chequers PH turn L uphill on track 'Bridleway'

7 Fine track. At fork after 800 m (½ mile) bear left (blue arrow)

8 Climb steeply through woodland. Shortly after exit from woodland at 'Pound Pond' sign turn L on broad track along field edge (blue arrow)

9 Follow downhill through wood. At T-j with road R steeply uphill then 1st L sharply back on yourself onto concrete track 'Bridleway, Harecramp Farmhouse'

10 Go past farm. At T-junction of tracks at bottom of hill by 3-way white arrows R then after 100 m (yd) L through metal bridlegate 'Harecramp Estate, Bridleway'

11 Steep climb through field between wooden posts then along woodland track. At T-j with road R

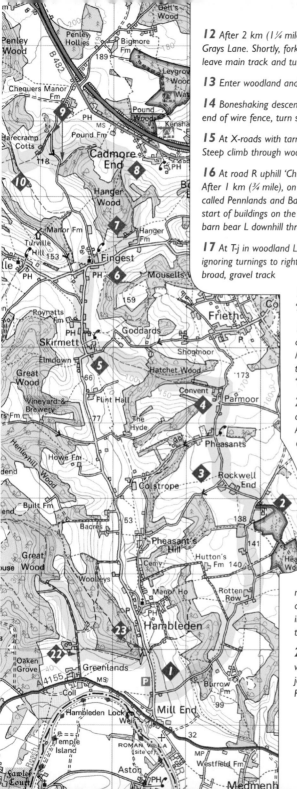

12 After 2 km (1¼ mile) turn L opposite telephone box onto Grays Lane. Shortly, fork R onto track. After 400 m (¼ mile) leave main track and turn R along rough field edge

13 Enter woodland and turn L on broad track

14 Boneshaking descent. Shortly after exit from wood, at the end of wire fence, turn sharp L following fence around corner

15 At X-roads with tarmac lane diagonally L onto grassy track. Steep climb through woodland. At T-j with track L uphill

16 At road R uphill 'Christmas Common 1¼. **Easy to miss.** After 1 km (¾ mile), on exit from woodland, shortly after houses called Pennlands and Badgerbury on the left and opposite the start of buildings on the right, turn L 'Bridleway'. At red-brick barn bear L downhill through field

17 At T-j in woodland L. Long descent following white arrows, ignoring turnings to right and left. Surface improves to fine, broad, gravel track

18 At road R. At T-j with B480 L 'Assendon 2½, Henley 4 3/4'

19 **Easy to miss.** After 800 m (½ mile) and shortly after passing a right turn to Maidensgove, turn L onto narrow grassy track opposite flint and red-tile house 'Bridleway'

20 Track improves. Very steep climb alongside fence. At T-j with track at top L. At T-j with road on sharp bend bear L (in effect SA). Superb views to the right.

21 After 2 km (1¼ miles) the road turns sharp R. After further 400 m (¼ mile) turn L by Woodend Farm. At end of concrete track bear R onto woodland track (white arrow)

22 Follow down through woodland then open farmland for 4 km (2½ miles). The first section may be rough/muddy but as you continue downhill the track broadens and surface improves. Shortly after red-brick house on the right next track L 'Bridleway'

23 Follow main track close to RH edge of woodland, eventually bearing R at fork to join road near house. At T-j with road turn R to return to start

3 Woodland tracks and the Grand Union Canal in southwest Hertfordshire

For an area so close to the large centres of population of Hemel Hempstead, Rickmansworth and Amersham, this ride has a very rural, wooded feel to it. From the centre of Bovingdon you soon leave tarmac for a woodland track that runs past a golf course and before long drops down onto the towpath of the Grand Union Canal through Kings Langley. You pass underneath the M25 on the towpath and then over it as you climb from Hunton Bridge up towards Commonwood. The avenue of trees as soon as you cross the motorway and go off-road seems to welcome you to a different world from the traffic mayhem you have just passed over. Permissive bridleways, tiny lanes and unclassified roads take you down into the valley of the River Chess near Chenies. A 3 km (2 mile) stretch through woodland is followed by a complete contrast: two busy road miles. Push hard for ten minutes and you are back off-road again, climbing towards Ley Hill along Broomstick Lane. A last off-road section, which may at times be rough takes you to within a mile of Bovingdon and the start.

1 Take the minor road between the Bull PH and the half-timbered house away from the centre of Bovingdon. After 400 m (¼ mile) opposite the corner of the cemetery, R onto track 'Unsuitable for motors'

2 Easy to miss. After 1½ km (1 mile) (track has become tarmac), just after sharp LH bend and a sign for Shothanger Way, leave the road and turn R uphill onto track by sign for Berry Wood, taking the LH fork after 10 m (yd)

➡ **three pages**

14 At T-j by triangle of grass L 'Chenies' then 1st track R 'Bridleway'. After 400 m (yd) at T-j of tracks L

15 At X-roads of tracks SA downhill onto narrower track. At 2nd X-roads of tracks SA downhill ('No Horses' signs to right and left). Maybe muddy

16 At bottom of hill L through gate (blue arrow) onto better track alongside the stream. Follow through farm. At T-j with road R. At T-j with more major road by large triangle of grass L

17 1st road R by large triangle of grass. At T-j R 'Amersham 4½' then after 50 m (yd) on sharp LH bend R 'Great House Farm access. Bridleway'

18 After 100 m (yd) at T-j R, then after 100 m (yd) L through black metal gate opposite concrete drive

19 Superb track. At road R, then L onto upper, narrower track 'Sporting rights reserved'

20 State of track is variable. At road with 'Forest Cottages' ahead R. At T-j at bottom of Bell Lane L 'Chesham 3'

21 Easy to miss. After 3 km (2 miles) on this busy road, past the sign at start of Chesham, and 200 m (yd) past car showroom on your right, R onto Hill Farm Road 'Bridleway to Botley'. As road swings sharp right bear L steeply uphill onto tarmac track 'Bridleway to Botley'

Bovingdon   Felden   Rucklers Lane   Kings Langley

22 Shortly after start of descent, at X-roads of tracks L gently uphill

23 At T-j with more major track R gently uphill 'Bridleway'

24 At offset X-roads at the end of Bottom Lane SA onto Broomstick Lane (or right for Five Bells PH)

25 At T-j at end of Broomstick Lane R. Just after sharp LH bend by the Swan PH leave the road and turn L onto track (**or** to avoid muddy section do **not** leave road but follow for 2½ km (1½ miles) and rejoin at instruction 28 '...just before chevrons').

26 Track bears downhill and to the left. At times muddy. At T-j with tarmac track R

27 Exit via gate, turn R. Just before joining the road R onto track through wood. Starts rough but soon improves

28 At X-roads at Pudds Cross at the end of Pocketsdell Lane turn L. After 800 m (½ mile), just before chevrons, R onto Green Lane 'Bovingdon Green' to return to the start

93

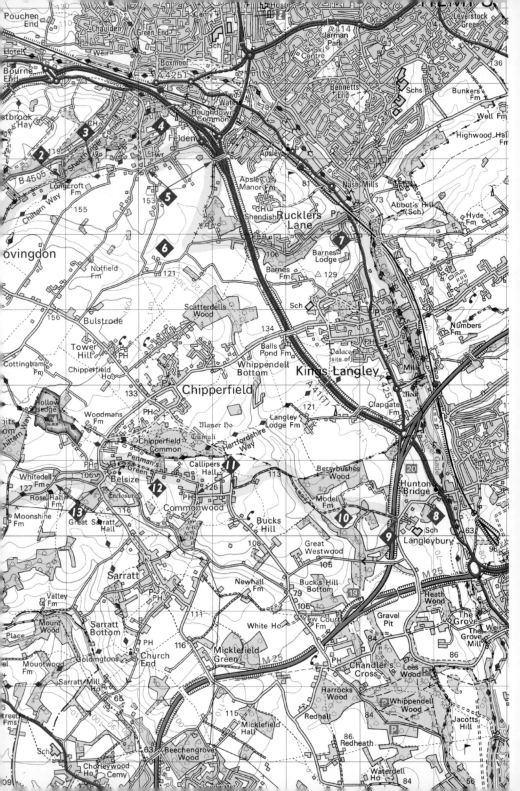

2 Easy to miss. After 1½ km (1 mile) (track has become tarmac), just after sharp LH bend and a sign for Shothanger Way, leave the road and turn R uphill onto track by sign for Berry Wood, taking the LH fork after 10 m (yd)

3 At 1st X-roads of tracks SA. At 2nd X-roads / T-j (with tyres on ropes ahead) L downhill on broad track, then just beyond white fence by Gosnells turn R 'Bridleway'

4 Follow this track alongside the golf fairway. At X-roads with the road through the golf course SA 'Bridleway'. At T-j with road R

5 At X-roads at the end of Felden Lane L onto Featherbed Lane 'Apsley 1'. After 1 km (¾ mile), just before crossing bridge over A41, R onto track 'Bridleway'. At times muddy

6 At T-j with road L

7 At traffic lights at the end of Rucklers Lane by the railway bridge L then R. Cross the bridge over the canal and turn R onto towpath

8 Follow towpath for 4 km (2½ miles). It changes sides and goes beneath the M25. At the round-arched brick bridge no. 162, with a sign for the Dog and Partridge PH, leave the towpath and turn R onto the road. At X-roads with the A41 SA onto Langleybury Lane

9 After 800 m (½ mile), shortly after passing a turning on the left to Langleybury School, next R onto tarmac lane and bridge over M25 'Public Footpath'

10 At black and white timber farm building, leave tarmac on a sharp RH bend and bear L (in effect SA) on to track

11 Fine track turns to tarmac. At T-j with road L then R onto Quickmoor Lane. After 800 m (½ mile) on sharp LH bend by Cart and Horses PH R onto No Through Road 'Penman's Green'

12 After 1 km (¾ mile), as road swings sharp left to Hillmeads Farm, SA onto track 'Permissive Bridleway'

13 Follow in the same direction as it improves near to houses and becomes concrete track. At T-j with road near the Plough PH L onto the major road 'Dunny Lane. Poles Hill' then after 300 m (yd) sharply R onto Bragmans Lane. At T-j L (NS)

 three pages

Start

The Bull PH, Bovingdon, 5 km (3 miles) southwest of Hemel Hempstead

P No specific car park. Please park with consideration

Distance and grade

35 km (22 miles)
 Moderate

Terrain

61 m (200 ft) climb from the Grand Union Canal at Hunton Bridge to Commonwood. 79 m (260 ft) climb from Latimer to Ley Hill. Lowest point – 64 m (210 ft) Grand Union Canal at Hunton Bridge. Highest point – 160 m (530 ft) at Pudds Cross near Bovingdon

Nearest railway

Kings Langley (on the route), Little Chalfont (just south of the route near Latimer)

Refreshments

Bull PH, Bell PH, **Bovingdon** Rose and Crown PH ♥, **Kings Langley** Cart and Horses PH, **Commonwood** The Plough PH, **Belsize** Bricklayers Arms PH ♥♥, **Hogpits Bottom, Flaunden** (just off the route) Red Lion PH ♥♥, **Chenies** Five Bells PH, **Cowcroft** The Swan PH ♥♥, The Crown PH, **Ley Hill**

4 ◆ *Through woods and hills between Tring and Berkhamsted*

Although Tring and Berkhamsted may seem two somewhat improbable centres for off-road cycling in Hertfordshire, there are many fine bridleways through the woods above the two towns, and if all else fails, the Grand Union Canal with its generally well-maintained towpath runs between them. The ride leaves Tring to the east, crosses the canal and soon joins an excellent stretch of improved bridleway. If only it were all of this quality! You climb up on to Aldbury Common and around the edge of Northchurch Common. There is an abrupt change of scenery as you pass from wooded bridleway straight into the centre of Berkhamsted. You soon climb out of the town, under the new bypass and head off-road to the ruins of Marlin Chapel. A lovely disused county road through woodland drops you on the road that runs through Cholesbury. From here, you climb to the highest point of the ride at Hastoe and the best descent of the day back to Tring.

Start

The car park in the centre of Tring, on the High Street. (Alternatively, the Sports Centre in Berkhamsted)

P As above

Distance and grade

27 km (17 miles)

Moderate / strenuous according to the conditions underfoot

Terrain

Two major climbs out of the valley through which the Grand Union Canal passes. The first of 79 m (260 ft) from Tring Station to Aldbury Common, the second of 120 m (400 ft) steeply at first then more gradually from Berkhamsted to Hastoe on the edge of the escarpment above Tring. Lowest point – 110 m (360 ft) in Berkhamsted. Highest point – 230 m (780 ft) at Hastoe

Nearest railway

Tring or Berkhamsted

Tring

Aldbury

Berkhamsted

Places of interest

Tring 1
Small market town with Zoological Museum crammed with hundreds of stuffed species. Tring Reservoirs National Reserve is home to many water birds including the great crested grebe, heron and pochard

Berkhamsted 12
Country town on the Grand Union Canal where William the Conqueror accepted the English throne in 1066. The Norman Castle was a favourite royal residence until the time of Elizabeth I – it is now in ruins

Hertfordshire mud is renowned for its sticky, cement-like quality. Although every attempt has been made to use tracks that are passable for a large part of the year, you are likely to encounter mud at various points and this will be much worse from late autumn to late spring and after any particularly wet periods. Wear appropriate footwear and hose your bike down after use. Should you wish to cycle away from traffic on easier tracks, try the Grand Union Canal towpath or the dismantled railways listed in the introduction

Refreshments

*Plenty of choice **in Tring and Berkhamsted**
The Valiant Soldier PH , The Greyhound PH ,
Aldbury (just off the route)
The Full Moon PH, **Cholesbury***

Heath End

Cholesbury

Hastoe

1 Turn L out of the car park. At the roundabout SA then 1st L on to Station Road 'Tring Station'.

2 After 800 m (½ mile), shortly after X-roads sign, L on to Grove Road. After 800 m (½ mile) 1st road R onto Marshcroft Road 'No Through Road'

3 Tarmac becomes track. At T-j with road R then after 200 m (yd) L onto Bridleway between the fence and the hedge. At offset X-roads with track, R then L along lower edge of wood (i.e. keep wood to your left)

4 Carry on in same direction as track improves just inside the woodland. At X-roads of bridleways SA. At road bear L

5 After 400 m (yd), on sharp LH bend, bear R onto track. At T-j with road R (ignore tempting track ahead: it soon deteriorates into a steep muddy push)

6 After 1 km (¾ mile) L onto a good track towards barn with corrugated roof 'Bridleway'. Past barn, through gate into field then diagonally L across field towards signpost and into the wood via a wooden gate 'Bridleway'

7 Continue in the same direction through several gates and through farm. Track improves. At T-j with road on steep bend R uphill

8 Easy to miss. Ignore 1st muddy bridleway on right after 400 m (¼ mile). After further 800 m (½ mile), just past the timber building of 'Chiltern Base Camp' and a clearing on your left, and 300 m (yd) before the road junction, turn R through a rough car park

9 You will eventually exit the wood and arrive at the edge of Northchurch Common. Turn R along the track that borders the wood, keeping the wood on your right as the track swings round to the left

10 Emerge at road opposite Hill Farm. Turn R for 200 m (yd) then L onto Bridleway. Take the track that leads away from the road bearing L and slightly uphill. At the T-j with driveway leading to Northchurch Farm L then R just before farm. At better track by Long Acre bear R

11 At T-j with tarmac lane by triangle of grass SA onto track in woodland 'Bridleway'. The track runs along parallel with the houses to your right. Emerge in a housing estate and go SA downhill on road called 'Bridleway'

12 At T-j with Bridgewater Road R then L down Billet Lane. At traffic lights at the end of Billet Lane, cross the main road and go SA between railings towards the Sports Centre

13 At T-j just past Sports Centre at the end of Douglas Gardens L then at X-roads by 'Stop' sign at the end of Shrublands Road R uphill on to Cross Oak Road

14 Steep climb. At X-roads at the end of Cross Oak Road SA on to Denny Lane. 200 m (yd) after passing underneath bridge R through wooden gates on to concrete track

15 At end of concrete track L on to stone track. 50 m (yd) short of the chapel ruins bear L 'Public Bridleway'. Cross new plantation of trees diagonally L to the far corner. Muddy patch near gate. Turn L onto track.

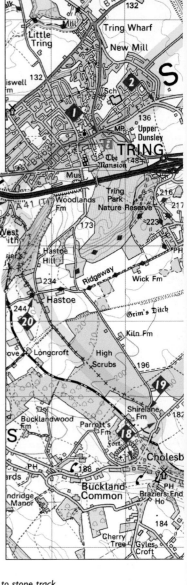

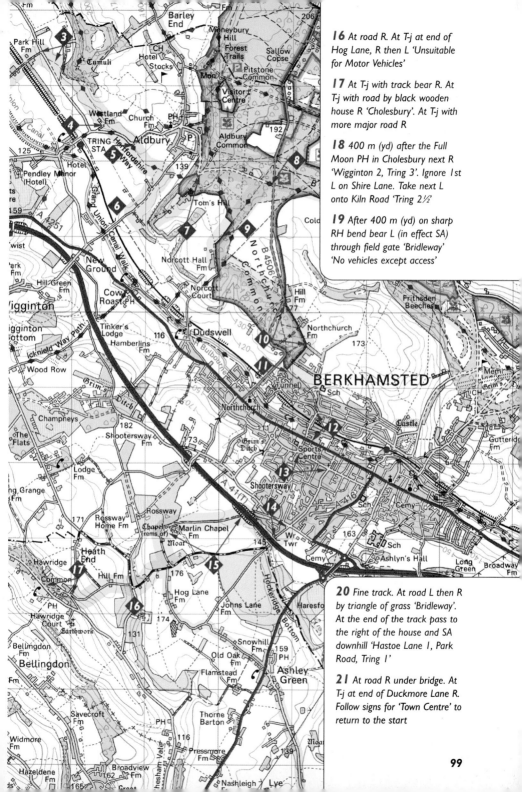

16 At road R. At T-j at end of Hog Lane, R then L 'Unsuitable for Motor Vehicles'

17 At T-j with track bear R. At T-j with road by black wooden house R 'Cholesbury'. At T-j with more major road R

18 400 m (yd) after the Full Moon PH in Cholesbury next R 'Wigginton 2, Tring 3'. Ignore 1st L on Shire Lane. Take next L onto Kiln Road 'Tring 2½'

19 After 400 m (yd) on sharp RH bend bear L (in effect SA) through field gate 'Bridleway' 'No vehicles except access'

20 Fine track. At road L then R by triangle of grass 'Bridleway'. At the end of the track pass to the right of the house and SA downhill 'Hastoe Lane 1, Park Road, Tring 1'

21 At road R under bridge. At T-j at end of Duckmore Lane R. Follow signs for 'Town Centre' to return to the start

5 ◆ *Tracks through the Chilterns between Wendover and Chesham*

A steep climb out of Wendover takes you to the top of Coombe Hill, one of the highest points in the Chilterns. You descend from the ridge into the valley of Hampden Bottom before climbing again to Prestwood. An off-road descent to Little Missenden is followed by quiet lanes that take you almost as far as Chesham, before heading in a generally northwest direction over Lee Common. Passing out-of-the-way country pubs, you climb to a 230 m (750 ft) high point above Wendover, which leaves you with a 3 km (2 miles) descent back to the start.

▲ Bacombe Hill

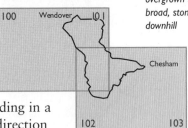

1 From the clock tower head west towards the railway station. Continue onto Pound Street then over the bridge that crosses the railway and the A413

2 400 m (yd) after crossing railway bridge, on sharp RH bend with chevrons L 'Public Bridleway. Ridgeway'. At sign for Bacombe Hill fork L 'Horses and mountain bikes'

3 Muddy near top. Emerge at car park. At T-j with road L

4 Short, steep hill. At X-roads in Dunsmore by pond R onto No Through Road 'Public Bridleway'

5 Past Black Horse restaurant. Single track section is muddy. Views to the right. Another muddy section created by horses. At road SA onto track 'Public Bridleway'

6 Follow track in same direction as it changes surface between gravel, tarmac and earth. Short, muddy or overgrown section before descent on better, broad, stony track. Join tarmac and continue downhill

7 At T-j at end of Mapridge Green Lane L, then after 400 m (¼ mile) 1st road R on Broombarn Lane

8 At X-roads at end of Broombarn Lane SA onto Green Lane. At T-j by yellow hydrant L (NS)

9 At T-j at the end of Naird Wood Lane R. After 400 m (¼ mile) at Peterley Manor Farm L on broad tarmac drive that soon becomes track

➡ two pages

Wendover Low Scrubs Dunsmore Prestwood Holmer Green

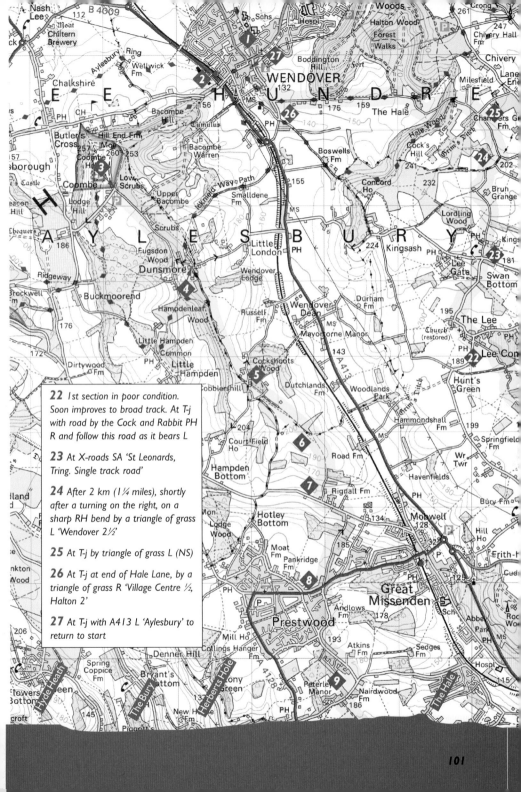

22 1st section in poor condition. Soon improves to broad track. At T-j with road by the Cock and Rabbit PH R and follow this road as it bears L

23 At X-roads SA 'St Leonards, Tring. Single track road'

24 After 2 km (1¼ miles), shortly after a turning on the right, on a sharp RH bend by a triangle of grass L 'Wendover 2½'

25 At T-j by triangle of grass L (NS)

26 At T-j at end of Hale Lane, by a triangle of grass R 'Village Centre ½, Halton 2'

27 At T-j with A413 L 'Aylesbury' to return to start

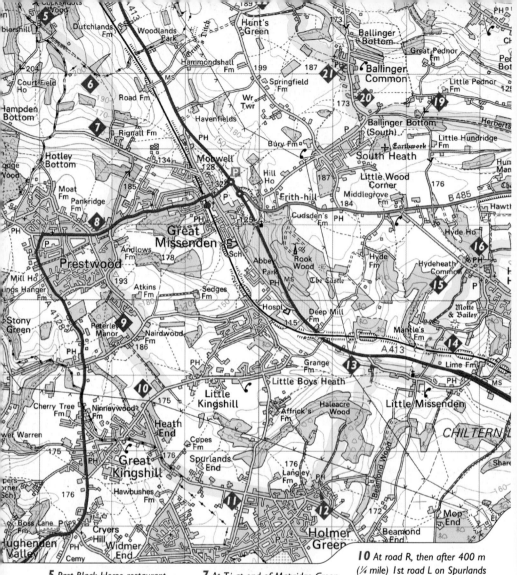

5 Past Black Horse restaurant. Single track 1st section is muddy. Views to the right. Another muddy section created by horses. At road SA onto track 'Public Bridleway'

6 Follow track in same direction as it changes surface between gravel, tarmac and earth. Short, muddy or overgrown section before descent on better, broad, stony track. Join tarmac and continue downhill

7 At T-j at end of Mapridge Green Lane L, then after 400 m (¼ mile) 1st road R on Broombarn Lane

8 At X-roads at end of Broombarn Lane SA onto Green Lane. At T-j by yellow water hydrant L (NS)

9 At T-j at the end of Naird Wood Lane R, then after 400 m (¼ mile) at Peterley Manor Farm L on broad tarmac drive that soon becomes track

10 At road R, then after 400 m (¼ mile) 1st road L on Spurlands End Road 'Holmer Green 1'

11 At double mini-roundabout by Mandarin Duck Bar at the end of Spurlands End Road SA onto Beech Tree Road

12 400 m (¼ mile) past village green and Bat and Ball PH, almost opposite Winters Way on your right L onto broad track 'Public Bridleway'. Starts

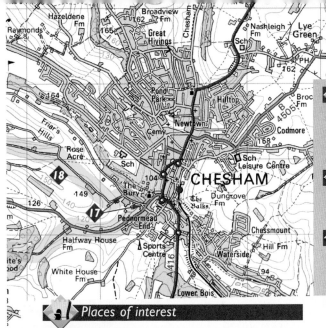

▷ Start

The clock tower,
Wendover

🅿 Railway Station

Distance and grade

20

36 km (22½ miles)
🗡🗡🗡 Moderate

Terrain

A mixture of small
lanes and tracks
through woodland, at
times narrow with
isolated muddy or
overgrown sections.
Two climbs: 120 m
(400 ft) from
Wendover up Bacombe
Hill and 91 m (300 ft)
from Chesham to St
Leonards above
Wendover

Nearest railway

Wendover, Great
Missenden, Chesham

🚶 Places of interest

Coombe Hill 2/3

At 260 m (852 ft), Coombe Hill is one of the
highest points in the Chilterns. It has magnificent
views over the neighbouring ridges and the Vale of
Aylesbury. The monument perched on the hillside
commemorates those Buckinghamshire men who
died in the Boer War. Down to the east lies
Chequers, a mid-16th-century mansion with ball-
topped gables; it was given to the nation in 1921 by
Lord Lee of Fareham as a country home for Prime
Ministers.

unpromisingly, at times wonderful, at
times passable

13 At road R, then 1st L after
church. At offset X-roads with A413
R, then L onto Chalk Lane 'Single
Track Road'

14 400 m (¼ mile) after going under
railway bridge, on sharp RH bend by
triangle of grass L on No Through
Road 'De Fontenay. Public Bridleway'

15 At T-j at end of Bullbaiters Lane
R. At end of village green, just past
PO/stores on the right and wooden

bus shelter on left L on tarmac lane/
track 'Public footpath and bridleway'

16 After 300 m (yd) with double
metal gates ahead turn R along
track. At T-j with busy road (B485) R

17 Opposite Queens Head PH L on
Church Street, then at T-j L again.
Immediately after The Bury Farm L
on Drydell Lane

18 After 1½ km (1 mile), shortly
after passing a small wood on the
left, on sharp RH bend at bottom of
hill L by double wooden gates

'Herberts Hole. Bridleway. CM7.
South Heath. Chiltern Link'

19 Follow blue arrows and 'Chiltern
Link' signs along valley bottom. At
road SA

20 At T-j by triangle of grass R
'Ballinger ½, Lee Common 1'

21 At Pheasant Inn PH opposite
Blackfield Lane L on No Through
Road 'Public Bridleway. St Mary's
Church'

◀ two pages

From Aldbury, along the Icknield Way and back through the woodland of Berkhamsted Common

The ride starts from the pretty village of Aldbury and lets you warm up with 5 km (3 miles) on road into Ivinghoe. The condition of the Icknield Way at this point is variable and may have been damaged by horses riding through in wet conditions. The church at Edlesborough, set dramatically on a small hill, represents the end of this section. A steep climb to Whipsnade follows. You have the alternative of cycling on the road or pushing/cycling off-road to reach the village of Whipsnade. Beyond Whipsnade, you once again face the choice of a rough 5 km (3 miles) off-road or a road alternative that may at times be busy. This is known as Hobson's choice! Beyond Hudnall, things improve with a combination of disused county roads (including an extraordinary section beyond the church in Nettleden between high flint walls and beneath a bridge). The ride soon reaches Berkhamsted Common and follows lovely woodland trails for almost 8 km (5 miles) back to Aldbury.

Start

The Greyhound PH, Aldbury, 5 km (3 miles) east of Tring, 16 km (10 miles) east of Aylesbury

P Some parking by the Greyhound PH close to the X-roads in Aldbury. Otherwise, park with consideration

Distance and grade

32 km (20 miles)
Moderate / strenuous according to conditions underfoot

Terrain

100 m (335 ft) climb from the Icknield Way to Whipsnade (one short but very steep off-road push to avoid the busy B4540). 61 m (200 ft) climb from the A4146 up to Hudnall. The steepest rideable climb is south from the church at

Aldbury

Ivinghoe

Edlesborough

The Valiant Soldier PH 🍺, The Greyhound PH 🍺, **Aldbury**
Rose and Crown PH, **Ivinghoe** The Bell PH, **Edlesborough**
The Plough PH, **at X-roads with B489**
Chequers Inn PH, **Whipsnade**
The Bell PH 🍺, Red Lion PH 🍺, **Studham**
(just off the route)
Alford Arms PH 🍺, **Frithsden**

Nettleden between amazing flint walls. Lowest point – 100 m (330 ft) on Icknield Way near to Edlesborough. Highest point – 210 m (700 ft) at Whipsnade

 Nearest railway

Tring Station, 1½ km (1 mile) west of Aldbury

Places of interest

Ivinghoe Beacon 4
One of several beacon points established during the reign of Elizabeth I to summon men in case of Spanish invasion

Whipsnade Zoo 11
Open air zoo on Dunstable Downs where 200 animals roam in the 500 acre park. Rarities include a herd of white rhinoceroses

Ashridge Park 23
The 32 m (108 ft) tall Bridgewater Monument was erected in 1831 in memory of the canal pioneer, the 3rd Duke of Bridgewater. On the eastern side of the park is the Gothic revival Ashridge House (now a college) set in gardens land-scaped by Capability Brown

▲ The Icknield Way near the church at Edlesborough

Studham   Great
                 Gaddesden   Frithsden

1 With back to the Greyhound PH L out of Aldbury on the road towards Ivinghoe

2 After 4 km (2½ miles) at T-j with B488 bear R downhill 'Ivinghoe ½, Dunstable 6, Leighton Buzzard 7'

3 Ignore the B488 to Dunstable. Take the next R in Ivinghoe onto Vicarage Lane, then 1st R by the Rose and Crown PH on to Wellcroft

4 Follow this in the same direction as it becomes track, at times muddy and pocked with horse hoofmarks. Join tarmac lane and continue in same direction

5 At X-roads with lane SA on to track towards church on hill

6 At X-roads by the church and the Bell PH in Edlesborough SA 'Village Centre' then 2nd R on to Pebblemoor by the Village Hall

7 At the end of the village on a sharp RH bend L onto lane (NS). 1st road R (NS). At T-j R (NS)

8 At roundabout (with B489) by the Plough PH SA 'Dagnall B4506, Whipsnade (B4540)' then 1st L onto B4540 'Whipsnade 1¼, The Zoo 1'

9 Shortly after a prominent Footpath sign on the left, turn L onto Bridleway. (This starts as a very steep push but avoids the busy road. If you wish to continue on the road, go SA as far as the Chequers PH and rejoin at 2nd part of instruction 11)

10 Shortly after passing a sign on your left to Dunstable Downs, at a X-roads with a broader track SA uphill. At the next track junction bear R then once in the field bear L following 'Icknield Way' sign

11 The track joins tarmac by a wooden gate. Follow to the road, turn L for 400 m (yd) then 1st R by triangle of grass towards the Chequers PH

12 Follow this lane along the edge of the fence around Whipsnade. After 800 m (½ mile) turn R onto bridleway following the fence on your right

13 At end of wood, carry SA along LH field edge. Go into wood and bear L onto superb, improved surface. It doesn't last long! At end of wood SA on to rougher track

14 At tarmac R then at T-j by letter box in brick pillar, R onto Valley Road. At T-j by triangle of grass R onto Common Road then after 300 m (yd) L onto track by 'Home Reddings' 'Bridleway'

15 Rough field edge. Descend on bumpy track to road. At road SA along field edge (check to see whether the track is better on the RH or LH side of the hedgerow. If you take the RH track you will need to cross back through the hedge via a gate after 400 m (yd). The bridleway swings uphill and left beneath the edge of the wood. Follow the track into the wood with a property to your right

16 At tarmac bear L. At X-roads with road by Little Gaddesden sign SA on to No Through Road

17 Tarmac turns to track then back to tarmac. At T-j sharply R steeply uphill

18 Fast descent. At T-j by church R then L 'Unsuitable for motor vehicles'. High brick and flint walls either side of the steep track

19 At T-j by the Alford Arms PH L. At T-j after 150 m (yd) R 'Potten End, Berkhamsted'

20 Steady climb. After 1 km (¾ mile), and 30 m (yd) after passing the first road turning to the left to Potten End, turn R onto Public Bridleway and take the RH fork

21 Follow this along the edge of the wood past the golf course. At road SA and continue in the same direction through woodland with the fairway on your left. The route is not always clear but as long as you avoid going onto the golf course and stay just on the border of the wood you should be on target

22 Go past Brick Kiln Cottage and continue in the same direction. At X-roads with a broad well-made track by a brick barn to the left SA

23 At X-roads with main road (B4506) R for 400 m (¼ mile) then L onto Bridleway opposite a small parking area in the woodland.

24 Continue in same direction until reaching property with National Trust sign. Carry SA for 400 m (yd). With the slope dropping away steeply ahead, bear R on broad track as it swings round contouring through the woodland.

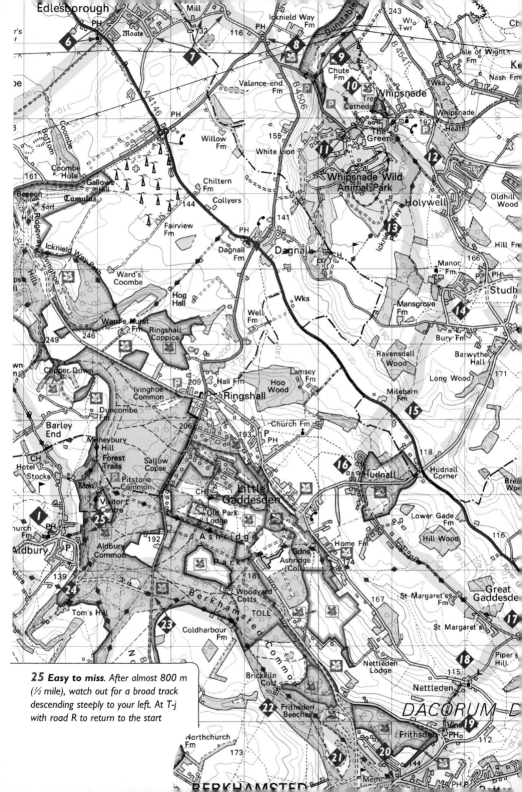

25 Easy to miss. After almost 800 m (½ mile), watch out for a broad track descending steeply to your left. At T-j with road R to return to the start

7 From Great Offley along the Icknield Way Path

Although it may seem a slightly unlikely centre, the village of Great Offley not only boasts four pubs and a restaurant but has within a 8 km (5 mile) radius of the village, dozens of miles of good-quality tracks ideal for off-road cycling, whether these be bridleways, byways or old, unclassified county roads that have fallen into a state of benign neglect. Most famous of these is the Icknield Way that runs from the end of the Ridgeway and connects with the Peddars Way, making it part of a track that used to run from Dorset to the Wash. The highest point of the ride is reached on the Icknield Way at the top of Telegraph Hill, which is followed by an enjoyable, gentle descent to the road. Hitchin is skirted on three sides before the lanes link up with an old county road that climbs over 91 m (300 ft) back to Great Offley.

Refreshments

Green Man PH ●●, Bull PH, Red Lion PH ●,
Prince Henry PH ●, **Great Offley**
Lilley Arms PH, **Lilley**
Cat and Fiddle PH ●, Motte and Bailey PH,
Fox PH, **Pirton**
Bird in Hand PH, Bull PH, **Gosmore**

Start

The Bull PH, Great Offley, just off the A505 between Luton and Hitchin

🅿 Visitors car park - with back to the Bull PH turn R for 300 m (yd) then 1st R onto Gosling Road, 1st L onto Clarion Close and 1st L again (alternatively, park in High Street, showing consideration)

Distance and grade

32 km (20 miles) (Short route - 16 km (10 miles)) Moderate (Short route-easy)

Terrain

64 m (210 ft) climb from Lilley Bottom to Telegraph Hill. 100-m (330 ft) climb from St Ippollitts back to Great Offley. Lowest point – 50 m (165 ft) at Ickleford. Highest point – 190 m (610 ft) on Telegraph Hill (Icknield Way)

Nearest railway

Hitchin, 1½ km (1 mile) from the route at the A505 between Hitchin and Letchworth

Great Offley

Lilley

Pirton

Icknield Way 5
Stretching from the Thames at Goring where it joins the Ridgeway, northeast to Thetford, where it joins the Peddars Way, the Icknield Way is part of a prehistoric trading route that ran from the Dorset Coast to the Wash

Lilley 3
Home of the 19th-century eccentric, Captain Dimpers, who claimed to be the last descendant of the medieval alchemists and to possess the secret of turning base metal into gold. The family crest of the Salusburys, local landowners, is carved on many of the cottages

Pirton 8
This was once a fortified village owing allegiance to a Norman knight named Stefan d'Arquelle who built a timber castle here, quite possibly on the site of prehistoric ramparts. The Motte and Bailey pub owes its name to the remnants of the Norman fortifications. The ghost of a headless horseman, a Cavalier named Simon Crossley, is said to ride around Midsummer's Day from the Elizabethan manor of High Down to Hitchin. During the Civil War he hid at High Down but he was caught and beheaded by the Roundheads

▼ East of Great Offley

Ickleford   Hitchin   Gossmore

1 With back to the Bull PH L. At X-roads at the end of High Street L 'Lilley'. 200 m (yd) after Prince Henry PH, on RH bend 1st L

2 At T-j with Lilley Bottom R 'Lilley, Hexton'

3 Just after church in Lilley, 1st L onto West Street

4 Tarmac becomes track. At X-roads of tracks SA. Just past start of golf course to your left, at major X-roads with better track, R (Icknield Way)

5 At T-j with road by Mortgrove Farm bear L (in effect SA). After 400 m (¼ mile) on sharp LH bend bear R into Treasures Grove Picnic Area 'Icknield Way'

6 Steady climb then fine gentle descent. At T-j with road R for 200 m (yd) (very busy – **take care**) then 1st track L along line of telegraph poles 'Bridleway' (**or for short route, turn R here onto broad track.** At T-j of tracks R to return to Great Offley)

7 At T-j of tracks at end of field R 'Bridleway. Icknield Way' (maybe muddy)

8 At junction with road SA '30 MPH'. At T-j with the Fox PH ahead R. At X-roads SA onto Hambridge Way

9 Easy to miss. Follow for 3 km (2 miles) (rough in parts). At junction of bridleways SA. 100 m (yd) before telegraph poles on the path (where the lines cross the track) R 'Bridleway. Icknield Way'

10 At road L 'Icknield Way'. At roundabout with A600 SA onto Turnpike Lane 'Ickleford, Arlesey'

11 Just past the church in Ickleford R onto track 'Icknield Way'. Cross the railway with **extreme care** (you will need to lift your bike over the gates)

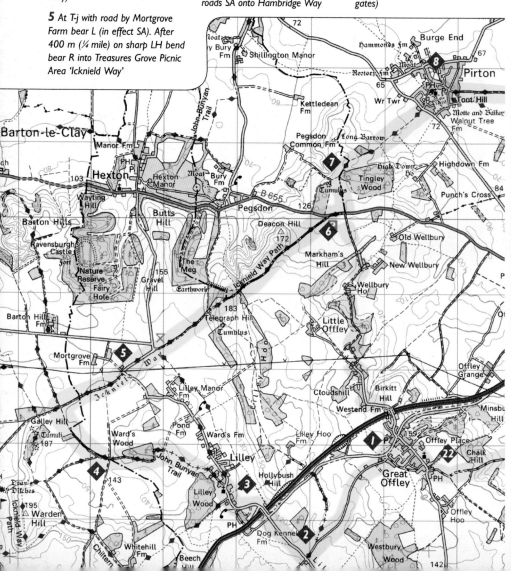

12 At T-j with road R

13 At roundabout SA onto Queenswood Drive. At X-roads SA onto Kingswood Avenue

14 At bottom of hill on sharp RH bend bear L (in effect SA) on to track

15 At X-roads with road SA 'Bridleway. Little Wymondley 1'

16 At T-j with road R. At roundabout R then L just before bus shelter onto track 'Bridleway'

17 Go under road bridge. **Easy to miss.** At the far end of field, just before going under power lines, as the track swings right, turn L over small bridge

18 At T-j with lane R. Just past church, by triangle of grass, L 'Gosmore, Preston'

19 At X-roads with B656 SA onto Waterdell Lane 'Gosmore'

20 At X-roads by the Bull PH SA onto Maydencroft Lane 'Unsuitable for HGV'

21 At T-j L. After 400 m (¼ mile) on sharp LH bend bear R (in effect SA) onto No Through Road 'Unsuitable for motors'

22 Follow in same direction, at times climbing steeply, to Great Offley. At T-j with road near the Red Lion PH R to return to the start

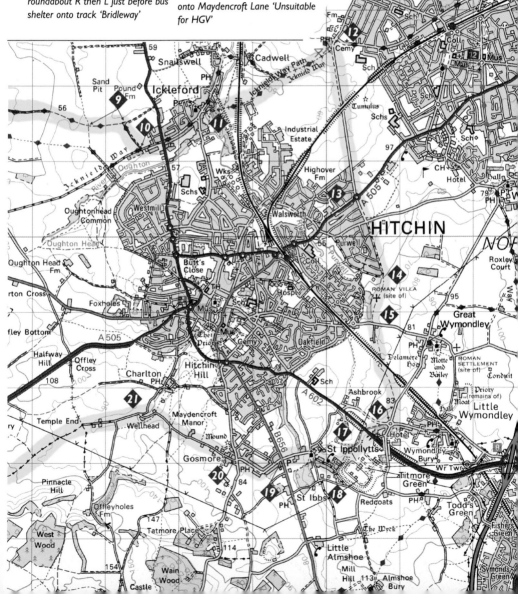

8 *Woodland tracks and a dismantled railway path southwest from Hertford*

Encircled by built-up areas running alongside the A1 and A10 and bounded to the north by the A414 and the south by the M25, there is a patch of countryside that offers many miles of fine off-road riding along broad gravel tracks through woodland. This short ride links together lanes and byways from the southwestern corner of Hertford through Brickendon to Newgate Street. The middle section runs along predominantly quiet lanes, including one that appears to have an identity crisis – it is signed 'Berkhamsted' on one side of the road and 'Berkhampstead' on the other! Just before Cole Green you find yourself at the start of the Cole Greenway, a magnificent conversion of an old dismantled railway line for recreational use that drops you right back at the start.

 Start

The car park next to Hertford Town Football Club, West Street, Hertford (just off the A414 Hatfield road past Hartwells car showroom)

P As above. Follow West Street for 400 m (yd). Shortly after the end of the houses on the left, turn R, on a LH bend, down a tarmac lane

 Distance and grade

22 km (14 miles)
Easy

 Terrain

61 m (200 ft) climb from the start to Brickendon. Lowest point – 42 m (140 ft) at the start. Highest point – 130 m (420 ft) at the start of Cucumber Lane

 Nearest railway

Hertford

Hertford

Brickendon

Newgate Street

Refreshments

*Plenty of choice in **Hertford***
*Farmers Boy PH, **Brickendon***
Coach and Horses PH, Crown PH,
Newgate Street
*Cowpers Arms PH, **Cole Green***

Hertford I

An attractive county town with many fine buildings faced with decorative plasterwork. Some of the most interesting are in Salisbury and Parliament Squares. The present castle is the 15th-century gatehouse to the now demolished Norman castle. The timber-framed Old Verger's House dates from 1450

Hatfield House *(8 km (5 miles) west of the route) 8* Superb red-brick Jacobean mansion built by Robert Cecil, 1st Earl of Salisbury, between 1607 and 1611 that boasts a Marble Hall, Grand Staircase and Long Gallery. The West Gardens have been re-created in 17th-century formal style

◀ *The knot garden at Hatfield House*

Little Berkhamsted

Letty Green

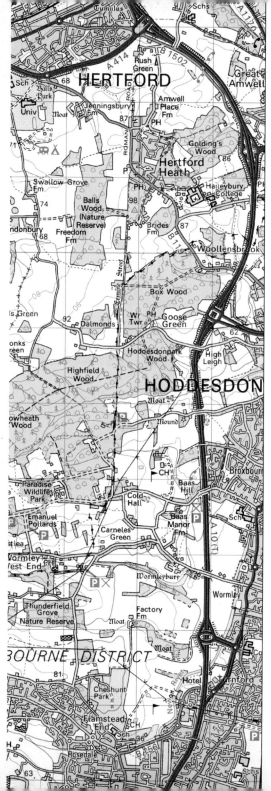

1 From the car park return to the road and turn R. At the roundabout SA onto Horns Mill Road then 2nd L onto Brickendon Lane 'Brickendonbury 1, Brickendon 2½'

2 *Easy to miss.* After almost 3 km (2 miles), after reaching the top of the hill, on a LH bend bear R by a large red-brick house onto a broad gravel track. Shortly, at fork of tracks, bear L

3 At T-j at the end of Fanshaw's Lane by the Farmer's Boy PH turn R

4 Shortly after crossing bridge over railway 1st L onto track 'Bridleway'. At black and white timber house bear R

5 At T-j with road by garden centre L then 1st R onto broad gravel track by red-brick lodge house

6 Track becomes tarmac. At T-j with road R then at roundabout SA. 1st L onto New Park Road 'No Through Road'

7 Follow as it turns to track and back to tarmac. At road L then 1st R onto Cucumber Lane 'Essendon'

8 After 2 km (1¼ miles) 1st R onto Berkhamsted Lane 'Little Berkhamsted'

9 Go down then uphill. Turn L onto track by white gates and lodge house 'Bridleway'

10 At bottom of hill L over stream then R onto broad gravel track

11 Continue SA through bridle gate. At X-roads at end of Bedwell Avenue SA 'Letty Green, Cole Green'

12 Just after passing beneath railway bridge and before Cowpers Arms PH turn R through car park and onto dismantled railway track

13 After 4 km (2½ miles) at 1st proper fork of tracks bear R (blue arrow on white circle) then L to go under railway viaduct and return to the start

9 Woods, lanes, streams and fords southeast of Stevenage

Southeast of Stevenage is a bewildering network of lanes and tracks. This ride links together a dozen off-road stretches with quiet lanes meandering in a lazy circle from Watton at Stone through the estates at Sacombe and Youngsbury to the first ford at the River Rib near to Cold Christmas. Fords can be very useful to the off-road cyclist to clean the bike of accumulated mud as well as providing some adventure in the crossing! The route follows the valley of the River Rib north towards Standon before turning west through High Trees Farm and Green End to the attractive village of Benington. A fine byway and a fast descent on a tiny lane bring you back to the start.

Start

The George and Dragon PH, Watton at Stone just off the A602 between Stevenage and Hertford

P Small car park near playing fields. Follow sign 'toilets' from opposite the Bull PH in Watton at Stone. Otherwise, near railway station or park in the main street showing consideration

Distance and grade

38 km (24 miles)
Moderate

Terrain

67 m (220 ft) climb from Stapleford to Sacombe Green. 61 m (200 ft) climb from the River Rib near to Latchford up to Levens Green. Lowest point – 48 m (160 ft) at Stapleford. Highest point – 120 m (400 ft) near Levens Green

Nearest railway

Watton at Stone

Watton at Stone

Stapleford

Sacombe Green

High Cross

Cold Christmas

Watton at Stone 1
The elegant, canopied, cast-iron pump dates back to the early 19th century

▲ *The neo-Norman gatehouse at Benington Lordship Gardens*

Much Hadham *(just off the route)* 13
Showpiece village, for centuries the country seat of the Bishops of London. Their palace, near the 12th-century church, is mainly Jacobean. The main street has many Elizabethan cottages and Regency houses

Benington Lordship Gardens 26
Hill-top gardens designed around an 18th-century manor house with Norman keep, which includes a rock, water and walled kitchen garden and magnificent display of roses. The village of Benington is one of the prettiest in Hertfordshire with all the right ingredients – church, folly, stately home, pub, timbered cottages, village green and duck-pond

Refreshments

George and Dragon PH, The Bull PH, Waggon and Horses PH, **Watton at Stone**
Woodhall Arms PH, **Stapleford**
Three Harts PH, **Stonyhills**
White Horse PH, **High Cross**
Ye Olde College Tavern PH, **Old Hall Green**
The Bell PH, **Benington**

Barwick   Latchford   Benington

1 With back to the George and Dragon PH L then after 300 m (yd) 1st L onto Station Road 'Watton Station, Datchworth'

2 Immediately after crossing railway bridge L then at T-j R onto No Through Road 'Bridleway'

3 At T-j with farm and barns ahead L then after 100 m (yd), just beyond gate bear L

4 At T-j L then after 200 m (yd) just before farm R onto track 'Bridleway. Stapleford 1½, Bramfield 1¾'

5 At T-j with road L. At T-j with A119 R 'Hertford' then 1st L 300 m (yd) after Woodhall Arms PH onto Church Lane 'Stonyhills 1'

6 At T-j with red-brick house ahead L

7 After 1½ km (1 mile), on LH bend bear R 'Ware'. At X-roads (with A602) SA on to tarmac drive 'Bridleway'. At farm leave tarmac, turn L over cattle grid between lodge and farm then 1st R

8 At fork of tracks just after big house L. At next fork by two ordinary houses L

9 At road R then R again 'High Cross'

10 After 3 km (2 miles) at T-j with A10 L then R onto North Drive 'Thundridge 1½, Wadesmill 1½, Ware 3½'

11 As lane swings right bear L through white gate onto track

12 At T-j with road L

13 After 3 km (2 miles), at T-j L 'Barwick'

14 **Easy to miss**. After 1 km (¾ mile), towards the bottom of the hill, 100 m (yd) before the ford, sharply R uphill onto track 'Bridleway'. After 400 m (¼ mile) as main

track swings right uphill bear L (in effect SA) onto narrower track in wood

15 At T-j with lane R. Ignore 1st left over bridge. As road turns right uphill bear L downhill between hedges

16 Tarmac becomes track. Take the middle track passing just to the R of round roofed low barn. Up and

down hill. At X-roads of tracks with field gate and bridle gate ahead, turn L

17 Exit field onto track by wooden barn. Bear L uphill. At X-roads with lane SA onto track 'Bridleway'

18 At T-j with road L. At T-j with A10 R (**take care** – busy road) then 1st L 'Old Hall Green'

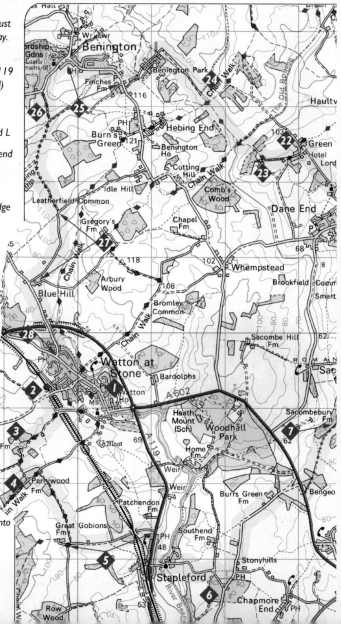

19 At T-j by Ye Olde College Tavern PH L 'Levens Green. Dane End'. After 1 km (¾ mile) 1st L onto No Through Road 'Beggarmans Lane. Dane End 1¾'

20 Through High Trees Farm. At T-j with road L. At T-j with more major road L 'Dane End' then 1st R 'Haultwick, Green End'

21 After 100 m (yd) L 'Green End. Hotel' then 1st R at triangle of grass by church 'Green End ½. Hotel'

22 Go past hotel. 50 m (yd) after passing pond on your right, as road swings left downhill, bear R onto track by triangle of grass 'Bridleway'

23 After 300 m (yd), leave main track and bear R onto rougher track. Fine descent. At bottom, cross bridge, turn L through metal gate then R along field edge

24 Exit at end of long field via bridle gate, turn L over small bridge then R along field edge. Track improves

25 Go through farm and past houses. At road R. In Benington, 200 m (yd) past the Bell PH L 'Aston, Stevenage'

26 After 800 m (½ mile), at bottom of hill L onto track 'Bridleway'

27 At T-j with road R then at T-j at bottom of hill L 'Watton'

28 At T-j at end of Walkern Road by the Waggon and Horses PH L to return to the start

10 *Tracks, lanes and the Icknield Way through undulating countryside southeast of Royston*

*T*his ride has a greater proportion of road than is usual for an off-road route but the lanes are quiet and scenic and the best section is left till last – a 8 km (5 mile) length of the Icknield Way. The route leaves the southwest of Royston and climbs 91 m (300 ft) to the mast on the A10 near to Reed. A bridleway east from Reed brings you to the most attractive village of Barkway with several old thatched buildings. Next, you pass through the estate of Cokenach with its fine house. A steady climb brings you past the squat square tower of Little Chishill church and onto the middle off-road section through woodland. Through Chrishall and just before Chrishall Grange, the route turns west along the Icknield Way for 8 km (5 miles) back to Royston.

Start

The Priory Church of St John Baptist, Royston, 19 km (12 miles) southwest of Cambridge

 Follow Melbourn Road (A10 towards Cambridge). At roundabout L onto King James Way and long-stay car park

Distance and grade

35 km (22 miles)

 Easy/moderate

Terrain

91 m (300 ft) climb from the start to crossing the A10 near Reed. 61 m (200 ft) climb to Little Chishill. 51 m (170 ft) climb on the last stretch of the Icknield Way just before Royston. Lowest point – 48 m (160 ft) on Icknield Way just to west of B1368. Highest point – 160 m (520 ft) on the A10 near to Reed

Nearest railway

Royston

Royston · Therfield · Reed · Barkway · Shaftenhoe End

Royston Cave 1
A unique bell-shaped chamber cut from the chalk beneath Melbourn Street, of unknown origin, but the carvings are

clearly medieval and most have religious and historical significance. It is believed to have been used by the Knights Templar before their proscription by the Pope in the 14th century (open in the afternoon on summer weekends)

▲ A carving in Royston Cave showing Saint Catherine

Barkway 8
Attractive village of thatched cottages dating back to the 17th century. Jacobean Manor Farm near to the 13th-century church. The village grew and prospered as a handy stopping place between Ware and Cambridge

Great Chishill (just off the route) 14
The showpiece of the village is the lofty 18th-century postmill, with white-painted timbers and a graceful fantail that turns the mill so that the sails always face the wind

Refreshments

Plenty of choice in **Royston**
Fox and Duck PH, **Therfield**
Cabinet PH 🍽, **Reed**
Tally Ho PH, Chaise and Pair PH, **Barkway**
Red Cow PH, **Chrishall**

Building End

Chrishall

Chrishall Grange

1 With back to the Priory Church L on the road towards Baldock. At traffic lights SA. Shortly after filling station on left L onto Briary Lane

2 Tarmac turns to track. Just past Lee Valley Water Works SA downhill onto rougher track

3 Track turns sharp R then sharp L. Follow blue arrows and signs for 'Icknield Way'. Ignore a stone track that crosses the grassy track and continue in the same direction

4 At top of steep hill bear R following blue arrows. Track becomes tarmac. At offset X-roads at the end of Mill Lane L 'Reed 2, Buckland 3¼'

5 At T-j with A10 R 'London' then 1st L onto Blacksmith's Lane 'Reed ½'. 1st R by telephone box onto Church Lane then 1st L onto Driftway

6 After 400 m (¼ mile) on sharp LH bend R onto tarmac track 'Public path to Barkway 1¼'. After 100 m (yd) 1st track L alongside hedgerow / trees

7 At T-j of tracks at the end of the field R and follow the main track as it turns L then R then L again to continue in the same eastwards direction. Rough middle section

8 Track improves. At T-j turn L downhill on good track that turns to tarmac. Go past church. At the end of Church Lane L

9 After 1 km (¾ mile) as the road starts to descend, 1st R onto lane/tarmac drive between brick-walled entrance to 'Cokenach'

10 Shortly after passing house and immediately after last of round green silos L onto track into wood

11 At the end of the wood, leave concrete track and turn L onto earth track

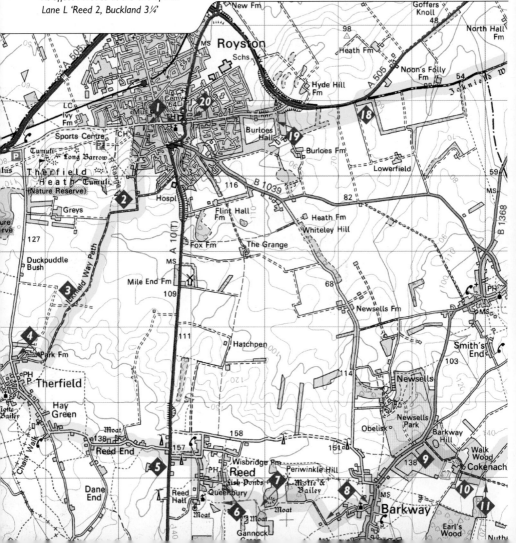

12 At T-j with road L

13 At T-j with Putty Hall Cottages ahead R 'Little & Great Chishill, Barley'

14 After 800 m (½ mile) at bottom of hill 1st road R 'Little Chishill ½, Langley 3'

15 Climb past church and spread-out barns of Gypsy Corner Farm. On sharp RH bend by beige brick house L 'Byway'

16 Short muddy section at far end of the wood. At road L. At T-j with B1039 R 'Audley End, Saffron

Walden' then 1st L 'Chrishall ½, Chrishall Grange 3½'

17 Easy to miss. 3 km (2 miles) after Chrishall, opposite a road turning to the right and just before a 'Chrishall Grange' sign, turn L onto track 'Bridleway. Royston 4¾. Icknield Way'

18 Follow this track in the same direction for 5½ km (3½ miles) over three X-roads with tarmac roads. 100 m (yd) before joining the noisy

and busy A505 turn L through wooden barrier 'Icknield Way'

19 This is variable in quality as it follows the field edge but passes through a lovely wooded section at the end. At T-j with tarmac drive R then after 20 m (yd) at T-j L

20 At 1st roundabout SA (**or** R onto King James Way for car park). At 2nd roundabout R to return to the start

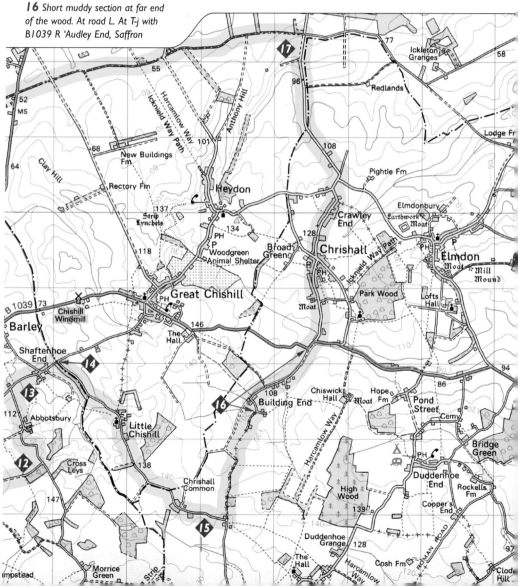

Byways and Roman Roads east from Fulbourn near Cambridge

The best is left till last in this ride with a 11 km (7 mile) section on the Roman Road of Worstead Street, which constitutes one of the finest stretches of off-road cycling in the whole of East Anglia: the track rises and falls on gently undulating country through a canopy of trees and among a carpet of wildflowers. The surface is excellent and it seems that the local authority has taken a real pride in maintaining this length to an exceptionally high standard. The ride starts from the bustling village of Fulbourn and heads northeast, then east along quiet lanes and byways to cross the A11 and the railway line. There is a remarkable sense of remoteness about parts of this ride, given its proximity to Cambridge. Turning south, the ride follows further byways through Balsham. At the second crossing of the B1052 you are faced with a decision – tea at the Chilford Hall Vineyard or straight ahead onto the Roman Road back to Fulbourn? With luck you should have time for both

 ## Start

The Church, Fulbourn, 6½ km (4 miles) east of Cambridge

🅿 Large car park at Fulbourn recreation ground behind the scout hut. From the Post Office go SA onto Manor Walk towards Balsham. Go past the Townley Memorial Hall and take the next L 'Fulbourn Institute'

 ## Distance and grade

37 km (23 miles)

🥾🥾 Easy

 ## Terrain

82 m (270 ft) climb from the start to Hungry Hill. Lowest point – 9 m (30 ft) just north of Fulbourn. Highest point 110 m (365 ft) just south of Balsham

 ## Nearest railway

Dullingham 3 km (2 miles) north of the route at Underwood Hall

Fulbourn

Cambridge Hill

Places of interest

Fulbourn 1
Reed-thatched houses line the streets of the village. The 13th-century church is only one of two in England dedicated to St Vigor. To the east of the village is Fleam Dyke, a massive 7th-century earthwork built to defend East Anglia against the Mercians

Great Wilbraham 2
In the 7th century, King Penda successfully marched against East Anglia and named this area after his daughter 'Wilburgh'

Swaffham Bulbeck (north of the route at Great Wilbraham) 2
A Dutch-style Merchant's House, granary and malt house remain from its 17th-century past as an inland port. The Italian portable altar in the 13th-century church is 500 years old. The pew-ends have 15th-century carvings of fabulous beasts

Refreshments

Six Bells PH, White Hart PH, **Fulbourn** Carpenters Arms PH, **Great Wilbraham** Black Bull PH, The Bell PH, **Balsham** Teashop at **Chilford Hall Vineyard** (just off the route between Balsham and Linton)

Chilford Hall Vineyard 15
18-acre vineyard with tours, wine tastings and a tea shop

Worsted Street (Roman Road) 17
A Roman link between the trading town of Cambridge and the major Roman Road from London (now the A11)

Wandlebury (just off the route southwest of Fulbourn) 18
The Gog Magog hills are crowned by an Iron Age fort whose ramparts enclose 15 acres. The hills take their name from a Romano-British giant who appears in legend, sometimes as one person, Gogmagog, sometimes as two, Gog and Magog. The nearby building is a stable block of the now-demolished mansion. The famous Arab stallion Elpappo was buried beneath the central arch in 1753

Balsham

Worsted Lodge

1 With back to the church R towards the Wilbrahams and Bottisham

2 Shortly after passing the Carpenters Arms PH in Great Wilbraham, on sharp LH bend R onto High Street then shortly R again onto Butt Lane

3 Pass around a metal gate 'No cars' then shortly fork L

4 At X-roads with road SA

5 At T-j with better track by telegraph poles R to cross A11 via bridge

6 At X-roads with road (A1304) SA 'Uneven crossing. Risk of grounding'

7 At X-roads R 'Six Mile Bottom 3, Weston Colville 3'

8 At X-roads SA 'Balsham 4, Linton 7'

9 After 1 km (¾ mile), on sharp LH bend shortly after double bend sign R onto track 'Byway. Icknield Way'. On bend by large blue storage tank bear L following telegraph poles

10 At X-roads with road SA 'Byway'

11 At X-roads with road by house and barn SA

12 Track becomes tarmac. At T-j with B1052 by triangle of grass with two trees turn L (**or** to avoid rough section, turn R on B1052 for 1½ km (1 mile) then R onto 'Roman Road Walk' and rejoin at instruction 15)

13 After 400 m (¼ mile), shortly after sharp RH bend by the Post Office (and before the Black Bull PH) R onto Woodhall Lane 'No Through Road' 'Icknield Way' (sections may be rough)

14 At T-j of tracks at the bottom of hill by telegraph poles turn R (sections may be rough)

15 At X-roads with road SA 'Byway' 'Roman Road Walk' (**or** L for tea at Chilford Hall Vineyard)

16 At X-roads with road SA

17 At T-j with A11 take the bridge over the road and continue in same direction

18 After 4 km (2½ miles), at T-j with road R

19 At X-roads at end of Shelford Road R onto Cambridge Road then after 150 m (yd) 1st L by triangle of grass 'The Wilbrahams' to return to the start

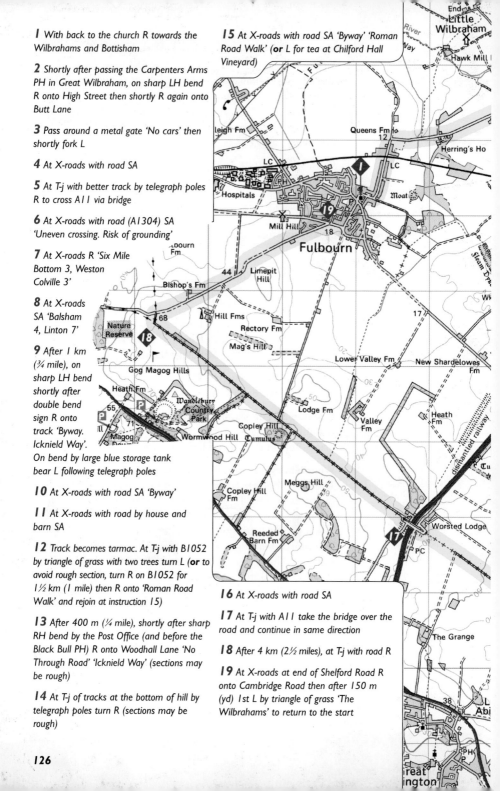

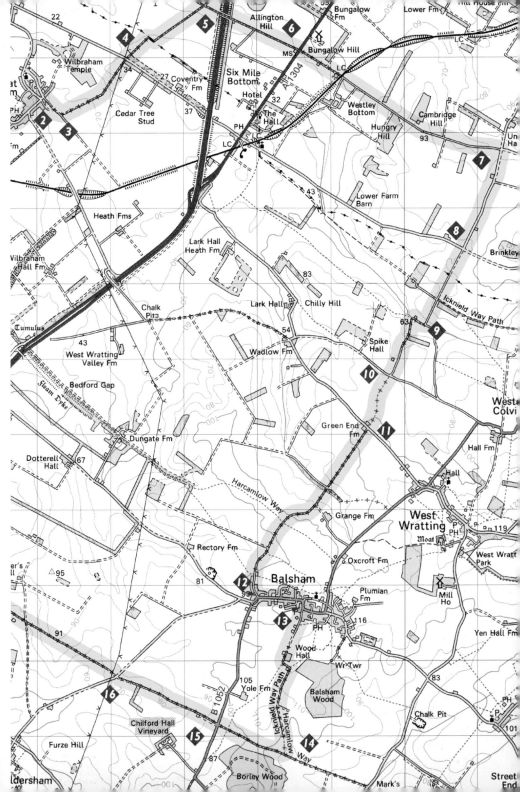

Useful addresses

British Cycling Federation
National Cycling Centre
Stuart Street
Manchester M11 4DQ
0870 871 2000
www.bcf.uk.com

The BCF co-ordinates and promotes an array
of cycle sports and cycling in general. They are
a good first point of contact if you want to find
out more about how to get involved in cycling.
The website provides information on upcoming
cycle events and competitions.

CTC (Cyclists Touring Club)
Cotterell House
69 Meadrow
Godalming
Surrey GU7 3HS
01483 417217
www.ctc.org.uk

Britain's largest cycling organisation, promoting
recreational and utility cycling. The CTC
provides touring and technical advice, legal aid
and insurance, and campaigns to improve
facilities and opportunities for all cyclists. The
website provides details of campaigns and
routes and has an online application form.

The London Cycling Campaign
Unit 228
30 Great Guildford Street
London SE1 0HS
020 7928 7220
www.lcc.org.uk

The LCC promotes cycling in London by
providing services for cyclists and by campaign-
ing for more facilities for cyclists. Membership
of the LCC provides the following benefits:
London Cyclist magazine, insurance, legal
advice, workshops, organised rides, discounts
in bike shops and much more. You can join
the LCC on its website.

Sustrans
Head Office
Crown House
37-41 Prince Street
Bristol BS1 4PS
General information line: 0117 929 0888
www.sustrans.org.uk

A registered charity, Sustrans designs and
builds systems for sustainable transport. It is
best known for its transformation of old
railway lines into safe, traffic-free routes for
cyclists and pedestrians and wheelchair users.
Sustrans is developing the 13,000 km (8000
mile) National Cycle Network on traffic-
calmed minor roads and traffic-free paths, to
be completed by the year 2005 with major
funding from the Millennium Commission.

Veteran Cycle Club
Membership Secretary
31 Yorke Road
Croxley Green
Rickmansworth
Herts WD3 3DW
www.v-cc.org.uk

A very active club, the VCC is concerned with
the history and restoration of veteran cycles.
Members enjoy organised rides and receive
excellent publications relating to cycle history
and club news.